CADOGAN CHESS BOOKS

Test Your Chess

Piece Power

CADOGAN CHESS SERIES

Chief Adviser: Garry Kasparov
Editor: Andrew Kinsman
Russian Series Editor: Ken Neat

Other titles for the novice player include:

LEV ALBURT
Test and Improve Your Chess

YURI AVERBAKH
Chess Endings: Essential Knowledge

JOSÉ CAPABLANCA
Chess Fundamentals

JULIAN HODGSON
Chess Travellers Quiz Book

DANIEL KING
How Good is Your Chess?

DANIEL KOPEC et al
Mastering Chess

STEWART REUBEN
Chess Openings – Your Choice

VLADIMIR VUKOVIC
The Art of Attack in Chess

JOHN WALKER
Chess Openings for Juniors

SIMON WEBB
Chess for Tigers

BARUCH WOOD
Easy Guide to Chess

For a catalogue of CADOGAN CHESS books (which includes the
Pergamon Chess and Maxwell Macmillan Chess lists) please write to:
Cadogan Books plc, London House, Parkgate Road, London SW11 4NQ
Tel: (0171) 738 1961   Fax: (0171) 924 5491

Test Your Chess

Piece Power

J.N. Walker

To free your game exchange off some of your
opponent's men . . . if possible, for nothing

Captain Joseph Bertin, 1735

CADOGAN CHESS
LONDON, NEW YORK

CADOGAN BOOKS DISTRIBUTION

UK/EUROPE/AUSTRALASIA/ASIA/AFRICA
Distribution: Grantham Book Services Ltd, Isaac Newton Way,
Alma Park Industrial Estate, Grantham, Lincs NG31 9SD.
Tel: (01476) 67421;   Fax: (01476) 590223.

USA/CANADA/LATIN AMERICA/JAPAN
Distribution: Paramount Distribution Center, Front & Brown Streets,
Riverside, New Jersey 08075, USA.
Tel: (609) 461 6500;   Fax: (609) 764 9122.

First published 1980 by Oxford University Press.

This edition published 1995 by Cadogan Books plc, London House,
Parkgate Road, London SW11 4NQ.

Offset from the Oxford University Press edition of Test Your Chess: Piece
Power. *Reprinted by kind permission of Oxford University Press.*

British Library Cataloguing in Publication Data
A CIP catalogue record for this book is available from the British Library.

ISBN 1 85744 185 0

Cover design by Artisan Design Factory, High Wycombe.
Printed in Great Britain by BPC Wheatons Ltd, Exeter.

Acknowledgements

In the preparation of this book more than 500 games and positions had to be tested for suitability and over a thousand questions answered and graded for difficulty before the final selection of 16 Testgames and 64 Problems could be made. No doubt the latest sophisticated scientific computer techniques could have done the job in five minutes. It took me over a year using the age-old, and probably more reliable, technique of slave labour! Namely William Gardner and Paul Fitches. Considering the colossal amount of work undertaken they would be entitled to feel their names should appear alongside mine on the cover and on the royalty cheque. Hard luck boys! You do know though that you have my deepest thanks for all that work, *and* for checking and rechecking the proofs so patiently, *and* for assisting with the paste-up, *and* for generally livening up the proceedings.

My thanks also to Nicholas Suckling for the arduous task of preparing the bulk of the diagrams, and to Stephen Everett and countless other boys of St Swithun's and Matthew Arnold Schools who contributed along the way.

As usual, thanks to Adam Hart-Davis who supplied most of the ideas, all of the inspiration, and who appears to have rewritten great chunks of the text at the editorial stage — which explains why we had such a job making it all fit neatly and tidily on the pages! My thanks also to Adam for the extensive use of his chess library and, in passing, to the greatest of all chess authors, Irving Chernev, who wrote most of the books in Adam's library.

Finally thanks to the 'Fair Maiden of First Steps', and her many rivals, for allowing my chief assistant time off from his other *duties*!

Oxford   *J. N. Walker*
January 1995

Contents

Contents

Introduction – how to use this book

This book is designed to instruct, examine, and entertain.

Instruction

There are five sections: 'The quick kill', 'Open files and the enemy ranks', 'Diagonals and bishops', 'Raiding knights', and 'Combined operations'. At the start of each section there are a few pages of general instructions telling you all you need to know before tackling the tests that follow.

Examination

In each section there is a series of tests split into two parts: 'Four problems to solve and Testgames'. The questions are all marked with a **Q**. After each question you will find a diagram showing the position and then the answer. If you cover your page with a sheet of paper or card, and lower it line by line as you read, there will be no danger of you seeing the answer before you solve the problem (unless you want to cheat of course!). The problems, testgames, and questions have been carefully graded to provide sixteen tests of equal difficulty. You will score 15 points if you solve the four problems and a further 35 if you answer correctly all the testgame questions. You can jot your score down on the piece of paper as you go along, enter the total in the scorechart at the beginning of the book, and see how much progress you are making from test to test.

Entertainment

Each test is followed by a fun section: a couple of pages of light relief after the examination. This may be an unusual game, a fine study, or an amusing incident from chess history. Chess may be a battle, it may need concentrated, intelligent thought, but it is still a game and should be fun!

Notation

Throughout this book we use the long form of algebraic notation.

THE BOARD

Each row of squares across the board is called a *rank*, and is given a number starting from White's side.

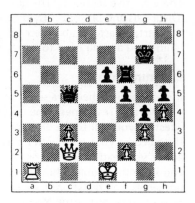

Each row of squares running up the board is called a *file*, and is given a letter starting from White's left hand side.

Each square is named by first giving the file letter and then the rank number. In our diagram the white rook stands at a1, the white queen at c2, the black king at g7, and so on.

THE SYMBOLS

We use symbols as abbreviations for pieces and chess terms.

K = king	**0-0** = castles on the K-side
Q = queen	**0-0-0** = castles on the Q-side
R = rook ♖	**x** = takes
B = bishop ♗	**-** = moves to
N = knight ♘	**+** = check (++ = double check)
The pawn (♙) has no symbol.	**e.p.** = en passant

We use **!** to show a good move, and **?** to show a bad move.

WRITING THE MOVES

There are four things to be written when recording a move.

(a) The symbol for the piece which moves (unless it is a pawn).

(b) The square it was standing on before moving.

(c) The action it makes.

(d) The square it moves to.

In the diagram opposite, the white rook which stands at a1 can move to a8 at the other end of the board. This would be written:

Ra1-a8

If check is given, the check sign is written after the move. In the diagram White can give check by playing his rook to a7:

Ra1-a7+

But then Black could capture the rook with his queen:

. . . Qc5xa7

As the pawn has no symbol the first of our four steps is left out when we write a pawn move. If White advances the pawn standing in front of his queen, the move is written:

c3-c4

NAMING PAWNS

A pawn is named after the file on which it stands. In the diagram, the pawn upon c3 is White's c-pawn (or queen's bishop's pawn). The pawn on e6 is Black's e-pawn (or king's pawn), and so on.

Some chess terms and expressions

RANK: a row of squares running across the board from left to right. The row from a1 to h1 is White's first rank.

FILE: a row of squares running from the white to the black side of the board. The a-file runs from a1 to a8; the b-file runs from b1 to b8, and so on. A pawn standing on a file belongs to that file; so the white pawn on a3 is the white a-pawn, and the black pawn on f7 is the black f-pawn.

K-SIDE: the half of the board to White's right: the e-, f-, g-, and h-files.

Q-SIDE: the other half of the board: the a-, b-, c-, and d-files.

OPEN FILE: a file on which neither side has a pawn. In the diagram the e-file and the h-file are both open.

HALF-OPEN FILE: a file upon which only one of the players has a pawn. In the diagram Black has two half-open files, the a-file and the d-file, while the c-file is half-open for White.

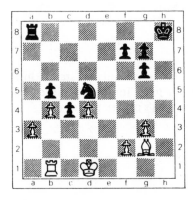

BLUNDER: a mistake.

DOUBLED PAWNS: when two pawns of the same colour are on the same file, they are said to be doubled. The black pawns on g7 and g6 are doubled on the g-file.

EN PRISE: a piece or pawn is said to be *en prise* when it is threatened. The black knight is *en prise* to the white bishop because Black has no way of recapturing if White plays Bg2xd5.

FIANCHETTO: a bishop is fianchettoed when the neighbouring knight's pawn has moved and the bishop is placed on its square. The white bishop on g2 is fianchettoed.

FLIGHT SQUARE: a square to which an attacked piece may run.

FORK: a double attack. If Black plays. . .Nd5-c3+ he is forking the white king and rook.

ISOLATED PAWN: a pawn is isolated when there is no pawn on the same colour on the files on either side of it. The white pawn on d4 is isolated because there are no white pawns on the e-file or the c-file.

LOOSE: undefended.

MAJOR PIECES: queen and rooks.

MINOR PIECES: bishops and knights.

OPENING: the part of the game when the pieces are being developed. This leads to the MIDDLE-GAME, where the forces properly join battle. The ENDING or ENDGAME is reached when one side will need to queen a pawn in order to give checkmate.

PASSED PAWN: a pawn is passed when it can advance to the eighth rank to queen without being either blocked or taken by an enemy pawn. The white pawn on d4 and the black pawn on c4 are therefore both passed, but the white pawn on a3 is not.

PIN: a piece is pinned when it cannot move without exposing a more valuable piece to capture. In the diagram, the white bishop pins Black's knight onto his rook.

SACRIFICE: giving up a piece or a pawn in the hope of gaining some kind of advantage.

THE EXCHANGE: the advantage of a rook against a minor piece. If in the diagram 1 . . .Nd5-c7 2 Bg2xa8 Nc7xa8, Black has lost the exchange.

Scorechart

	Page number	Test number	Four problems TOTAL (max 15)	Testgame TOTAL (max 35)	TOTAL (max 50)
The quick kill	6	1	9	25	34
	14	2	9	21	30
Open files and the enemy ranks	28	3	4	26	30
	36	4			
	44	5			
	52	6			
Diagonals and bishops	66	7			
	74	8			
	82	9			
	90	10			
Raiding knights	104	11			
	112	12			
	120	13			
	128	14			
Combined operations	138	15			
	144	16			

The quick kill

You cannot plan to win a game of chess in 15 moves. If you try to attack in the opening the most likely result is that your opponent will defend himself sensibly, stop your attack in its tracks, and then launch a strong and properly planned counter-attack. Even so, you must always be on the look-out for the chance of winning in the opening or early middle-game. All games are lost because of mistakes, and if your opponent goes wrong in the opening he may give you the chance you need. Apart from blundering and giving you a piece there are three main ways in which he can go wrong; three points for you to remember if you want to make that quick kill.

The weak f-square

The squares f2 for White and f7 for Black are the weak spots. At the start of a game each of these squares is right next to the king, and defended only by the king. This makes it a particularly good target for attack. Not only is there the chance of winning the f-pawn, but also the possibility of a direct attack and checkmate on the king.

The simplest form of the mating attack is the four move Scholar's Mate: **1 e2-e4 e7-e5 2 Bf1-c4 Nb8-c6 3 Qd1-h5 Ng8-f6 4 Qh5xf7 mate.**

Whilst this is not likely to happen in any of your games, it does show the most striking example of the weakness of the f-pawn square: the invasion complete and the black king sitting helpless. . .all by move 4!

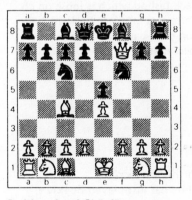

Position after 4 Qh5xf7 mate

Two other ways in which you can attack your opponent's weak square are the knight raid and the bishop sacrifice. You can try to get a knight on to the square, and fork your opponent's queen and rook. You can try to sacrifice a bishop on the square, and follow up with a combination regaining the piece. The three examples on the next page highlight the weakness of the f-pawn square.

The quick kill

The knight raid
White has just played Ng5xf7.
Black has allowed the knight to
get into his position; he has lost
his f-pawn and his queen and rook
are forked.

The bishop sacrifice
White has just played Bc4xf7+.
If the black king captures, White
will play Qd1-h5+ and win the
black bishop which is loose on c5.
White gets his piece back, he has
won the f-pawn, and Black can
never castle.

The bishop sacrifice
White has just played Bc4xf7+.
Black must capture with his king,
but when he does so he leaves his
queen unprotected, and White will
play Qd1xd8. White doesn't get his
piece back, but he does win a
queen!

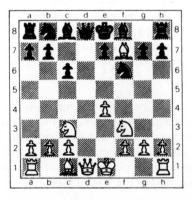

If your opponent fails to protect his weak f-square properly you may get the chance for a quick attack, but you must be careful. Don't go out of your way to attack the square if your opponent can defend it easily — you will only fall behind in development.

The open e-file

Early in a game pawns are often exchanged in the centre, particularly in openings which begin 1 e2-e4 e7-e5. When this happens a king can get into terrible trouble if he gets stranded at the end of an open e-file.

Here the black king has been caught in the centre by the white rook. The king must move to get out of check; he must give up the right to castle; he will have trouble finding a safe home.

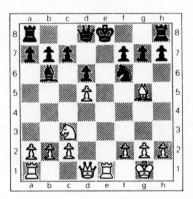

There are two other dangers to which a player exposes himself if he leaves his king on the end of the open e-file. One is a discovered check, the other is a pin.

The discovered check

Here the white knight will discover check when it moves off the open e-file.

The knight will go to c6 and Black, too busy saving his king, will lose his queen.

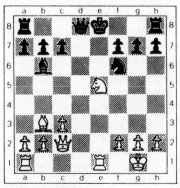

White to move

The quick kill

The pin

Here the white rook has just moved to e1, pinning the black knight to its king.

The knight cannot be saved. If Black defends it with a pawn, White will simply play d2-d3 next move.

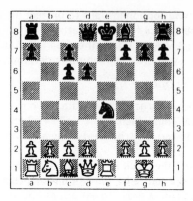

The collection of small errors

If one player makes several small mistakes in the opening, they may add up to give his opponent an attack. It isn't often that an international master gets himself mated in fourteen moves: here's one who did!

(*Sicilian Defence*)

Krogius	Ojanen
1 e2-e4	c7-c5
2 d2-d4	c5xd4
3 Ng1-f3	e7-e5
4 c2-c3	d4xc3
5 Nb1xc3	d7-d6
6 Bf1-c4	h7-h6

Now we have reached the position in the diagram. This is the point at which White realizes he has the chance of making a quick kill. . . the point at which Black starts getting bashed!

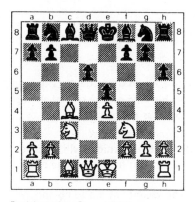

Position after 6 . . . h7-h6

7 Bc4xf7+! Ke8xf7
8 Nf3xe5+ Kf7-e7

Let's look at the other moves Black could have tried:

(a) 8 . . . d6xe5 9 Qd1xd8 costs him his queen.

(b) 8 . . . Kf7-e8 9 Qd1-h5+ Ke8-e7 10 Qh5-f7 costs him his king!

(c) 8 . . . Kf7-e6 9 Qd1-d5+ Ke6-f6 10 Qd5-f7+ also leads to mate.

(d) 8 . . . Kf7-f6 9 Qd1-d4 (threatening to win the black queen by 10 Ne5-c6+) Qd8-e8 10 Nc3-d5+ Kf6-e6 11 Nd5-c7+ and his queen falls.

9 Nc3-d5+   Ke7-e6
10 Qd1-g4+   Ke6xe5
11 Bc1-f4+   Ke5-d4
Or 11 . . .Ke5xe4 12 Nd5-c3+ Ke4-d4 13 Qg4-d1+ leading to mate.
12 Bf4-e3+   Kd4-e5
If 12 . . .Kd4-c4, 13 Qg4-e2 is mate.
13 Qg4-f4+   Ke5-e6
14 Qf4-f5 mate
There was no way Black could save himself after 7 Bc4xf7+; his position
was already lost after six moves! Why? Well, look at the diagram.

Two things are immediately obvious. White has three pieces in play;
Black has none. White's pieces attack and control the central squares;
Black's don't.

What did Black do wrong in his first six moves? Let's look at each
of Black's moves.

Move 1, . . .c7-c5 is the standard Sicilian Defence.
Move 2, . . .c5xd4 is the natural exchange.
Move 3, . . .e7-e5 is a greedy attempt to hang on to the extra pawn.
Move 4, . . .d4xc3 is the capture by which Black makes sure he keeps
    the extra pawn.
Move 5, . . .d7-d6 defends the e-pawn and opens the diagonal for a bishop.
Move 6, . . .h7-h6 stops White from playing Nf3-g5.

Not one of these six moves is a bad mistake, but put them together and
they add up to a lost position.

Black has: *Failed to develop his pieces.*
                Failed to control the centre.
                Wasted time with too many pawn moves.
                Wasted time pinching a pawn.
White has: *Developed sensibly.*
                Attacked the centre.

The result is that the white pieces were able to flow smoothly into the
attack while the black king could only stagger drunkenly around waiting
for the executioner.

The chance of a quick kill depends more upon your opponent than on
you. If he blunders or breaks the rules of the opening you may get your
chance. You must remember that your first job is to develop your pieces,
aggressively if possible, and to fight for the centre. Unless your opponent
goes wrong you cannot hope for more; only his mistakes will give you
the chance of a successful early attack — a quick kill.

TEST ONE

Four problems to solve

Here are four problems for you to solve. Each time read the question and set up the position on your board. *Don't read any further* until you have worked out your own answer to the question. You will find the correct answer immediately underneath the diagram. At the bottom of the page you will be told how many points you have scored if you solved the problem.

Q *White has neglected an important part of his development. How does Black punish him?*

Q *Black can win a pawn by playing 1 . . .Bc5xf2+ 2 Ke1xf2 Nf6-e4+. Can you find an even better move by which Black wins a bishop?*

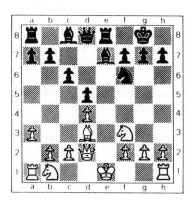

Black to move

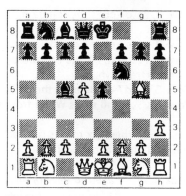

Black to move

The e-file is open and White has failed to castle. Black's rook is in position and he has a deadly discovered check:

1 . . . Be7-b4+

White's queen is attacked and he can't save her because he has to get out of check.

You score 2 points if you found this winning move.

White has wasted time with too many pawn moves and the piece he has developed is loose. Black hits White's weak square:

1 . . . Nf6-e4
2 Bg5-e3

If White captures the queen he is mated: 2 Bg5xd8 Bc5xf2.

2 . . . Bc5xe3

White has lost his bishop: if 3 f2xe3 Qd8-h4+ and mate next move.

Score 3 points.

Q *How does White make use of his advantage in space?*

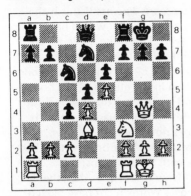

White to move

Q *White's pieces are well placed. How does he force checkmate?*

White to move

While developing his pieces Black has taken little care of his king. White destroys the castled position.

1 Bd3xh7+   Kg8xh7

If 1 . . .Kg8-h8, 2 Qg4-h5 wins.

2 Qg4-h5+   Kh7-g8
3 Nf3-g5

Threatening mate on h7.

3 . . .   Rf8-e8
4 Qh5xf7+   Kg8-h8
5 Qf7-h5+   Kh8-g8
6 Qh5-h7+   Kg8-f8
7 Qh7-h8+   Kf8-e7
8 Qh8xg7 mate

White's pieces had the freedom of the board!

Score 4 points.

Black has left f7 wide open:

1 Bc4-f7+   Ke8-e7

Black's king has lost the right to castle, but more important he is running out of places to go!

2 Qd4xf6+   Ke7xf6

If 2 . . .g7xf6, 3 Nc3-d5 is mate.

3 Nc3-d5+

The white pieces rule the centre of the board; they lure the black king to his doom.

3 . . .   Kf6-e5
4 Ng5-f3+   Ke5xe4
5 Nd5-c3 mate

Score 6 points if you found this brilliant winning line.

Testgame 1

Here is your first testgame. Play the moves on your board. Every few moves you will come to a question and a diagram of the position. Work out your own answer to the question before reading any further. Immediately after the diagram you will find the move actually played in the game, together with the number of points you may have scored.

(*Giuoco Piano*)

1	e2-e4	e7-e5
2	Ng1-f3	Nb8-c6
3	Bf1-c4	Bf8-c5
4	c2-c3	

White plans to set up a strong pawn centre.

4 . . .   **Ng8-f6**

Good development. Black brings his knight into play and attacks the white e-pawn.

Now here is your first question:

Q *Suppose you were White in this position. What move would you play?*

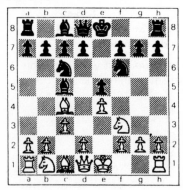

In the actual game White played:

5 d2-d4

You score 4 points if this is the move which you would have played. This is the move which White was planning when he played 4 c2-c3. It plants a second pawn in the middle of the board, and it opens up the diagonal for White's dark-squared bishop. It does not defend the e-pawn, but we will see later on how that fits in with White's plans.

Now what about the other moves White might have played?

You score 2 points if you would have played 5 d2-d3 to defend your e-pawn. This can't be a bad move, but it does make White's fourth move look rather silly. There is no point in 4 c2-c3 if White is not going to try to put a pawn on d4. After 5 d2-d3 White will have wasted a move, and his pawn on c3 will be in the way of his queen's knight.

Score 1 point if you would have played 5 Qd1-e2 or 5 Qd1-c2. Again you are defending your e-pawn, but you are committing your queen rather early in the game. Until a few more pieces are developed it won't become clear which is going to be the best square for the queen, and surely she must have more future than just defending the e-pawn. It is much better to leave the white queen on d1, where she is supporting the pawn push to d4.

Score 1 point for 5 0-0.

Score no points if you would have played any other move. Now, play the move 5 d2-d4 on your board and we will carry on with the game.

5 ...   e5xd4
6 c3xd4

Now c3 is open again for the white knight.

6 ...   Bc5-b4+
7 Nb1-c3   Nf6xe4

White's e-pawn has fallen. Normally it is wrong to move a piece twice in the opening; normally it is wrong to pinch a pawn in the opening. Here it is safe for Black to break these opening principles since it is a centre pawn he has pinched, a pawn which could have helped White's pieces get a big advantage in space in the middlegame.

. Now for the next question:

Q *What move do you think White should play now?*

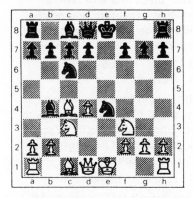

8 0-0

Score 4 points for this move.

When White played 5 d2-d4 he already knew he was going to sacrifice his e-pawn. He hoped for three things as compensation: (a) an advantage in space, (b) better development, and (c) the chance to catch the black king on the open e-file. Now White presses on with his development and prepares to bring his rook to e1.

Score 1 point for 8 Qd1-e2 or 8 Qd1-d3, but score nothing for other moves.

8 ...   Ne4xc3
9 b2xc3   Bb4xc3?

Now Black is being very greedy. By grabbing a second pawn he gives White the chance to swing into the attack.

Q *What should White do now?*

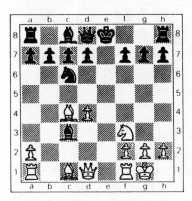

10 Bc1-a3

Score 4 points.
The bishop comes to life and prevents Black from castling. White isn't worried about his rook since the black royal family are in an

awful mess after 10 . . .Bc3xa1 11 Rf1-e1+ Nc6-e7 12 Ba3xe7.

Score 4 points for 10 Qd1-b3 which is equally good.

Score 1 point for 10 Ra1-b1.

No score for 10 Qd1-e2+. Black would escape from check by 10 . . . Qd8-e7, and there is no way that White wants to exchange queens.

10 . . .   d7-d6

Black shuts the bishop's diagonal.

Q *What should White play now?*

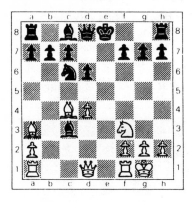

11 Ra1-c1

Score 3 points.

Aggressive development. White saves his rook, puts it on a good file, and gains time by attacking the black bishop.

Score 1 point for 11 Ra1-b1.

11 . . .   Bc3-a5
12 Qd1-a4

Once again we have development with gain of time. White threatens 13 d4-d5 winning a piece. Black

must meet the threat: he doesn't have time for a developing move.

12 . . .   a7-a6

Now if 13 d4-d5, Black plays 13 . . .b7-b5.

Q *How does White continue his attack?*

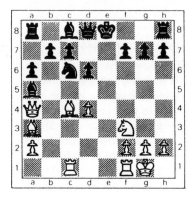

13 Bc4-d5

Score 4 points.

Another attacking move which makes Black lose time. White threatens to capture first on c6, and then on a5. Black must save his bishop.

13 . . .   Ba5-b6
14 Rc1xc6!

White could have regained one of his pawns if he had captured with the bishop: 14 Bd5xc6+ b7xc6 15 Qa4xc6+, but he gets no more after 15 . . .Bc8-d7.

14 . . .   Bc8-d7

Black daren't take the rook: 14 . . .b7xc6 15 Qa4xc6+ Bc8-d7 16 Qc6xa8 and he comes out a piece down.

Q *How does White improve his position?*

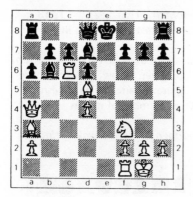

15 Rf1-e1+

Score 5 points.

White seizes the open e-file.

15 ...   Ke8-f8
16 Rc6xd6!   c7xd6

If 16...Bd7xa4, 17 Rd6xd8 is mate.

17 Ba3xd6+   Kf8-g8

Q *Now what should White play?*

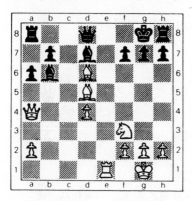

18 Nf3-g5

Score 6 points.

White attacks the weak f-square. He threatens 19 Bd5xf7 mate.

Score 4 points for the sacrifice 18 Bd5xf7+ which also gives White a good attack.

Score 3 points for 18 Nf3-e5. This also threatens mate at f7, but blocks the e-file.

Score 2 points for 18 Qa4-b3 or 18 Qa4-c4.

18 ...   Bd7-e8

If 18...Qd8xg5 19 Qa4xd7 and Black can't stop both the mates threatened (on e8 and f7).

Q *How does White finish off his opponent?*

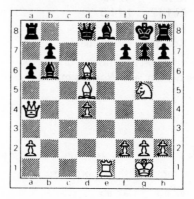

19 Re1xe8+!

Score 5 points.

Score 5 points for 19 Qa4xe8+! which is just the same.

19 ...:   Qd8xe8
20 Qa4xe8+   Ra8xe8
21 Bd5xf7 mate

Now add up the points you have scored and enter the total in the score chart facing page 1.

How quickly can you...?

How quickly can you checkmate your opponent? That's easy! **1 f2-f3 e7-e5 2 g2-g4 Qd8-h4 mate.** Two moves; the fastest checkmate in the west!

Here are four more quickies for you to have a go at. . .just for a bit of fun. Try each one before you look at the solution given below. You may have to play some ridiculous moves and make up crazy games! That doesn't matter; just complete the task in the quickest number of moves.

How quickly can you checkmate your opponent if your checkmating move has to discover check?

The record for this one is just four moves. White kindly marches his king out into the open. . .and Black clobbers him:

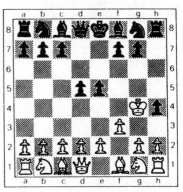

1	f2-f3	e7-e5
2	Ke1-f2	h7-h5
3	Kf2-g3	h5-h4+
4	Kg3-g4	d7-d5 mate

The d-pawn has moved, uncovered the bishop, and White is mated.

Position after 4 . . . d7-d5 mate

How quickly can you play a game ending in stalemate?

Ten moves is the record here:

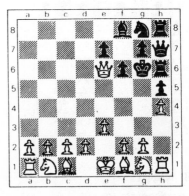

1	e2-e3	a7-a5
2	Qd1-h5	Ra8-a6
3	Qh5xa5	h7-h5
4	Qa5xc7	Ra6-h6
5	h2-h4	f7-f6
6	Qc7xd7+	Ke8-f7
7	Qd7xb7	Qd8-d3
8	Qb7xb8	Qd3-h7
9	Qb8xc8	Kf7-g6
10	Qc8-e6	Stalemate!

There was some pretty bad chess played in that game!

Position after 10 Qc8-e6 stalemate

How quickly could you play a game in which all the pieces are exchanged?

You have got to end up with a position like the one in the diagram, with just two kings on the board. You will have done well if you can do it in anywhere near 20 moves: the record is just 17:

1	c2-c4	d7-d5
2	c4xd5	Qd8xd5
3	Qd1-c2	Qd5xg2
4	Qc2xc7	Qg2xg1
5	Qc7xb7	Qg1xh2
6	Qb7xb8	Qh2-e5
7	Qb8xc8+	Ra8xc8
8	Rh1xh7	Qe5xb2
9	Rh7xh8	Qb2xa2
10	Rh8xg8	Qb2xd2+
11	Ke1xd2	Rc8xc1
12	Rg8xg7	Rc1xb1
13	Rg7xf7	Rb1xf1

14	Rf7xf8+	Ke8xf8
15	Ra1xa7	Rf1xf2
16	Ra7xe7	Rf2xe2+
17	Kd2xe2	Kf8xe7

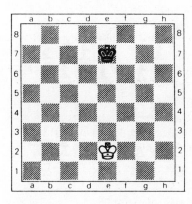

Position after 17 . . .Kf8xe7

How quickly could you play a game in which you capture all your opponent's men and leave your own set up ready for the start of a game?

The record for reaching a position like the one in the diagram is 16 moves:

1	Nb1-c3	b7-b5
2	Nc3xb5	Ng8-f6
3	Nb5xa7	Nf6-e4
4	Na7xc8	Ne4-c3
5	Nc8xe7	c7-c6
6	Ne7xc6	Nc3-b1
7	Nc6xb8	Ra8-a3
8	Nb8xd7	g7-g5
9	Nd7xf8	Qd8-d6
10	Nf8xh7	Ke8-e7
11	Nh7xg5	Rh8-h4
12	Ng5xf7	Rh4-c4
13	Nf7xd6	Ke7-f6
14	Nd6xc4	Kf6-f7

15	Nc4xa3	Kf7-e8
16	Na3xb1	

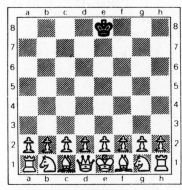

Position after 16 Na3xb1

TEST TWO

Four problems to solve

Q *How does White make use of his better development?*

Q *White has tried to attack too early. How does Black punish him?*

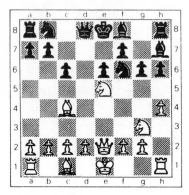

White to move

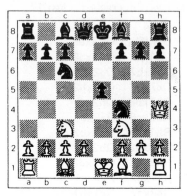

Black to move

The white pieces power down the centre; the breakthrough comes at Black's weak point.

1 Ne5xf7

White captures a pawn and forks the black queen and rook.

1 ...	Ke8xf7
2 Qe2xe6+	Kf7-g7
3 Qe6-f7 mate	

Score 2 points.

The white queen has come into play on an open board far too soon. She becomes a target for attack.

1 ...	Bf8-e7
2 Qh4-g3	Nf4-h5

Trapped! The queen has paid the price. . .there is nowhere left to go.

Score 3 points.

Q *The white king is stuck in the centre. How does Black finish him off?*

Q *Black's position is not as solid as it looks. How does White force checkmate?*

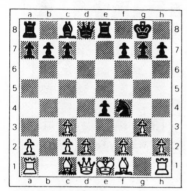

Black to move

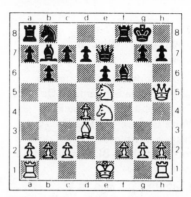

White to move

Black needs to open the e-file so that his rook can get at the white king.

1 ...   **Nf4-d3+**

White now has three moves: three ways of losing!

(a)
2 Ke1-e2   **Bc8-g4+**

When he loses his queen.

(b)
2 Bf1xd3   **e4xd3+**
3 Ke1-f1   **Bc8-h3+**
4 Kf1-g1   **Qd8-d5**
5 f2-f3   **Qd5-c5 mate**

When he loses his king.

(c)
2 c2xd3   **e4xd3+**
3 Bf1-e2   **Re8xe2+**

When he must give up his queen to avoid mate: if 4 Ke1-f1 Bc8-h3+ 5 Kf1-g1 Qd8-d5 etc.

Score 4 points.

White's well-placed pieces and advantage in space enable him to launch a sharp king attack.

1 Qh5xh7+   **Kg8xh7**
2 Ne4xf6++   **Kh7-h6**

If 2 ...Kh7-h8, 3 Ne5-g6 is mate.

3 Ne5-g4+   **Kh6-g5**
4 h2-h4+   **Kg5-f4**
5 g2-g3+   **Kf4-f3**

The king has no choice; he has to keep marching.

6 Bd3-e2+   **Kf3-g2**
7 Rh1-h2+   **Kg2-g1**
8 0-0-0 mate

White has completed his development in a useful way!

Score 6 points if you found this marvellous winning line.

Testgame 2

(*Ruy López*)

Balla	Réti
1 e2-e4	e7-e5
2 Ng1-f3	Nb8-c6
3 Bf1-b5	f7-f5

Black chooses a risky opening variation, the Schliemann Defence. The general idea of attacking White's centre can't be bad, but this is a pawn move which does nothing to help Black's development.

4 d2-d3	Ng8-f6
5 0-0	Bf8-c5

Black is developing his forces speedily.

6 Bb5-c4

The main trouble with Black's opening strategy is that when he played 3 . . .f7-f5 he opened the diagonal from a2 to g8, making it difficult for himself to castle and cover the weak point at f7. White does the natural thing – he puts a bishop on the diagonal – but in order to do so he wastes valuable time. He has already moved that bishop once!

6 ...	d7-d6
7 Nf3-g5?	

White can't resist having another bash at f7. He forgets all about his development. His Q-side pieces look on like statues as his king's knight moves for a second time. White has forgotten that development comes first, attack comes second.

Q *White threatens a knight fork on f7. What does Black do about it?*

7 ...	f5-f4!

Score 4 points.

Black does nothing about the fork! He realizes he will have to give up his rook, but he also realizes that a lead in development will give him the chance to attack.

Score 2 points for 7 . . .Qd8-e7 or 7 . . .Rh8-f8.

8 Ng5-f7	Qd8-e7
9 Nf7xh8	

Q *What should Black play now?*

9 ...   Bc8-g4

Score 4 points.

Excellent development. The bishop takes up a fine position and gains time by attacking the white queen. Now all Black's minor pieces are in play, and he is ready to begin the offensive.

Score 1 point for 9 . . .Nf6-g4, which opens the way for the queen to come to h4 and gives Black some sort of attacking chances. However, it blocks the queen's bishop and stops Black from throwing the full weight of his forces into the attack.

10 Qd1-d2

White is having to pay the price for his greed. He has spent four moves winning the rook. Now, when he wants to be completing his development, he is having to waste more time grovelling around with his queen.

Q *How does Black strengthen his attack?*

10 ...   Nc6-d4

Score 5 points.

Black has given up a rook. He has compensation in four ways:
(a) He has better development.
(b) His pieces attack and control more of the centre.
(c) White's position is cramped.
(d) White has only the pawn shield to cover his castled position . . .which is precisely where the black pieces are heading!

White must not be allowed to sort out his problems; if he does, then Black will simply be a rook down. Black knows he must keep up the pressure. He threatens 11 . . .Nd4-f3+ because after 12 g2xf3 Bg4xf3 there is no way that White can prevent him from playing 13 . . .Nf6xe4 and bringing his queen across for a mating attack.

Score 2 points for 10 . . .0-0-0 or 10 . . . Nf6-h5. Sensible moves, but they allow White time to breathe!

11 Kg1-h1

Q *Now what does Black do?*

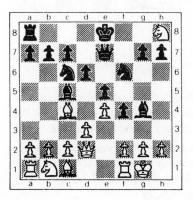

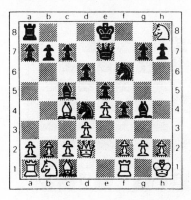

11 . . .   Nd4-f3!

Score 5 points.

The attack gets into full swing.
Black's plan is to destroy the pawn
shield protecting the white king.
He picks out h2 as his first target,
and saves time again by attacking
the white queen.

Score 3 points for 11 . . . Nf6-h5.

Score 2 points for 11 . . . 0-0-0. By
castling Black would complete his
development; but Black has two
sound reasons for not doing so:

(a) His king is safe where it is.
White has too few pieces in play
and no chance of opening the
centre files.

(b) The rook is not needed for the
attack. There are no open files on
the K-side for the rook to use, and
opening them would take Black too
much time.

12   Qd2-a5

He dare not take the knight: 12
g2xf3 Bg4xf3+ 13 Kh1-g1 Nf6xe4!

Q *What is Black's next move?*

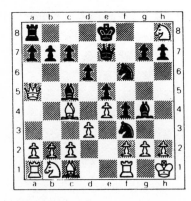

12 . . .   Nf6xe4!

Score 6 points.

Now the queen can join the attack.

Score 1 point for 12 . . .Nf6-h5.

13   g2-g3

White weakens his pawn shield; he
must stop the black queen from
going to h4. White can't take
either knight: (a) 13 g2xf3 Bg4xf3+
14 Kh1-g1 Qe7-g5 mate, or (b)
13 d3xe4 Qe7-h4 14 h2-h3 Bg4xh3
and again he is soon mated.

13	. . .	Ne4xf2+
14	Rf1xf2	Bc5xf2
15	Kh1-g2	

Q *What does Black do now?*

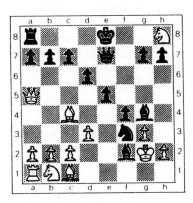

15 . . .   f4xg3

Score 3 points.

White's flimsy defences are ripped
apart; his king will have to face the
full fury of the black pieces.

Score 1 point if you were going to
move your dark-squared bishop to
b6, c5, d4, g1, or e1.

16   h2xg3

Q *Black's bishop is threatened again. What does Black do?*

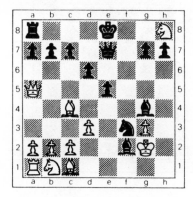

Q *How should Black escape from check?*

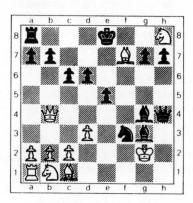

16 ...   Bf2xg3!

Score 4 points.

White's whole pawn shield has been viciously clubbed away. Now the foolishness of White's opening strategy is clear. The time wasted in attacking too soon, and greedily snatching the black rook, has cost him dearly. His Q-side pieces are useless, his remaining pieces are scattered like seed to the wind, and his king. . .his poor king has only the black pieces for company!

Score 1 point if you were simply going to save your bishop by moving it to b6, c5, d4, g1, or e1.

17 Qa5-b5+

White would have been mated immediately if he had taken the bishop: 17 Kg2xg3 Qe7-h4+ 18 Kg3-g2 Qh4-h2+ 19 Kg2-f1 Bg4-h3.

17 ...   c7-c6
18 Qb5-b4   Qe7-h4
19 Bc4-f7+

19 ...   Ke8-e7

Score 4 points.

The only move! With his own pieces clustered around the white king, Black will be able to force mate very soon. He must not get carried away with excitement; he must not forget that White is still playing. Any other move by the black king allows White too many checks.

20 Qb4xb7+ Ke7-f6

The king finds a safe home.

21 White resigns

White can win another rook, but he can't save his own king.

Black based his attack on sound aggressive development. He brought his pieces into play on good squares and steadily improved their positions, while at the same time he kept White busy answering nagging threats. White was never given time to complete his development.

A complicated position!

The position on the right appeared under the title 'A Complicated Position' in Richard Réti's book *New Ideas in Chess*. He then went on to discuss whether 1 e2-e4 is a better first move than 1 d2-d4. Réti said *'The opening is the hardest part of the game to play because it is very difficult at the beginning of the game to understand what is going on.'* On the battlefield the common soldier does the fighting after the general has made the difficult decisions

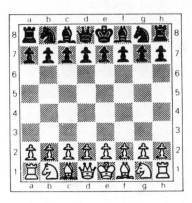

involved in studying the lie of the land and positioning his forces where they will be most effective. The chess player's job in the opening is the same as the general's. The chess player's opening moves will decide the shape of the chess battle to follow. The question of which is the best first move has caused a lot of argument:

Gyula Breyer set the ball rolling in the 1920s when he said *'After the first move 1 e2-e4, White's game is in its last throes!'*

Weaver Adams fired back by saying that after 1 e2-e4 *'White wins by force!'*

Paul Morphy didn't say anything. He didn't need to. In every single game he opened 1 e2-e4!

Bobby Fischer never played 1 d2-d4 in his career. He said *'The players of 1862 knew something very valuable that the players of today would do well to take note of: 1 d2-d4 leads to nothing!'*

Bill Hartston hit the nail properly on the head when he said *'Choosing between 1 e2-e4 and 1 d2-d4 is like choosing between tea and coffee.'* It's just a matter of which move is more likely to lead to positions which suit your own style and taste.

Richard Réti found his own answer to the argument. He championed his own opening, 1 Ng1-f3, and specialized in that and the English Opening, 1 c2-c4, for the rest of his life.

Think first, move later

Opening theory has been studied for centuries, and nowadays most masters can play the opening without any thought, moving almost automatically.

Moving automatically can be a dangerous business, as Alapin found to his horror when he played Dr Tarrasch at Breslau in 1889:

Tarrasch	Alapin
1 e2-e4	e7-e5
2 Ng1-f3	Ng8-f6
3 Nf3xe5	d7-d6
4 Ne5-f3	Nf6xe4

The game has begun with a standard Petrov Defence. Now Tarrasch *should* have played 5 d2-d4, the move always played in that position at that time. Tarrasch didn't!

5 d2-d3

Scarcely looking at the board Alapin instantly picked up his bishop to play 5 . . .Bf8-e7, Black's usual reply to 5 d2-d4. Only when he had bishop and hand hovering in mid-air did Alapin see his mistake. Too late he saw his knight was attacked. Too late, because once he had touched it he had to move that bishop.

Position after 5 d2-d3

If Alapin got a shock, how about Lindermann at Kiel four years later:

Lindermann	Echtermeyer
1 e2-e4	d7-d5
2 e4xd5	Qd8xd5

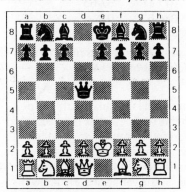

Lindermann now intended to play 3 Nb1-c3. But he picked up his queen's bishop by mistake. So what, you are thinking. Well in 1893 the rules of chess were slightly different. If you touched a piece and were unable to move it, you had to pay the penalty of moving your king. Lindermann had to play:

3 Ke1-e2

Position after 3 Ke1-e2

Now Echtermeyer has rather a good reply ready!

There is a moral here somewhere! *Think first, move later.*

Surprise, surprise!

Bobby Fischer never played 1 d2-d4. He always played 1 e2-e4. . .well, almost always. In the sixth game of his world championship match with Boris Spassky at Reykjavik in 1972 Bobby Fischer caused a sensation. Fischer played 1 c2-c4. Only twice before had Fischer ever played that move, and one of those times was in a game he knew he was going to win by default. For Spassky and his Russian seconds, who had no doubt spent many months studying Fischer's favourite opening variations, the sensation could not have been very pleasant! Fischer of course won the game.

Frank Marshall also realized the value of catching an opponent by surprise in the opening. In 1908 he worked out a tricky plan of counter-attack for Black against the Ruy López. Marshall didn't want to waste his shock weapon against just anybody. No, he wanted to catch somebody good with it; he wanted to win a famous battle, and he was prepared to wait. Frank Marshall did have to wait as well. Ten years in fact! It was at New York in 1918 that he got his chance against the great Capablanca.

(*Ruy López — Marshall Gambit*)

Capablanca	Marshall
1 e2-e4	e7-e5
2 Ng1-f3	Nb8-c6
3 Bf1-b5	a7-a6
4 Bb5-a4	Ng8-f6
5 0-0	Bf8-e7
6 Rf1-e1	b7-b5
7 Ba4-b3	0-0
8 c2-c3	

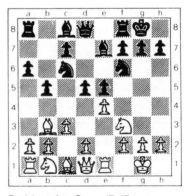

Position after 8 . . . d7-d5

And now Marshall pulled his new move out of the hat:

8 . . .	d7-d5

This made Capablanca think for a while! He knew that if he accepted Marshall's gambit he would have to face a terrific attack. He knew that Marshall must have spent hours studying all the variations. He knew his opponent was trying to take him by surprise. Even so, he felt his skill was being challenged. He could not run away from such a challenge. He must accept the gambit:

9 e4xd5	Nf6xd5
10 Nf3xe5	Nc6xe5
11 Re1xe5	Nd5-f6
12 Re5-e1	Be7-d6

And now Marshall had what he wanted: open lines, better development, and the attack. Unfortunately. . .he lost the game!

Open files and the enemy ranks

Rooks need open files. Shut a rook in behind your pawns and it's a lion in a cage, all life and energy with nowhere to strike. Swap off a few pawns and you have opened the door. The rook can spring into action, bound down the open file, and seize the enemy by the throat.

Files are opened when pawns are exchanged. You should open files by exchanging pawns when your pieces are in position to make use of the files, and your opponent's pieces are not. An open file is a motorway into the heart of the enemy position; you make use of it in three steps. First you control it with your pieces. Second you invade down it. Third you snipe sideways from it. The main targets of attack are the seventh and eighth ranks, the first two lines of the enemy position.

The eighth rank is a target when your opponent's king is castled and either shut in behind his own pawns, or unable to advance because your pieces attack the squares in front of him.

The white rook has invaded the back rank. The black king is trapped behind his own pawn shield. The rook snipes sideways and the king is mated.

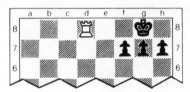

The eighth rank can also be used for firing at the enemy from behind.

The white rook has invaded the back rank and got in behind the black pawns. He can now move to right or left and attack them in the rear.

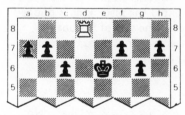

Sometimes the eighth rank can be used to give the enemy king a kick on the backside!

The white rook has used the back rank to steal up behind the black king.
Checkmate!

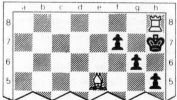

Both white rooks have seized the
eighth rank and the black king
has been hit from behind.
Checkmate again!

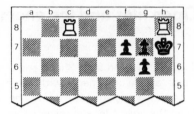

The seventh rank is a springboard from which you can snipe sideways at
the enemy pieces. Your opponent's pawns are the obvious target as they
start the game on that rank.

The white rook has invaded the
seventh and snipes sideways at the
enemy pieces. The black pawns
are sitting ducks; they cannot
defend one another from a sideways attack.

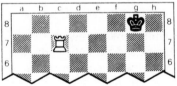

The seventh rank can also be used to trap your opponent's king against
the edge of the board.

The white rook has invaded the
seventh. The black king is trapped
against the side of the board,
since he cannot cross the rook's
line of fire.

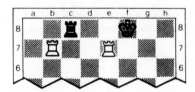

Two rooks on the seventh rank can be most dangerous. Apart from
supporting one another in sniping at the enemy men on the rank, they
can attack the enemy king with threats of checkmate and perpetual check.

The two white rooks control the
seventh and can go on giving
check for ever on that rank.
White can draw by perpetual
check. White can also move his
rook to h7 and threaten checkmate.

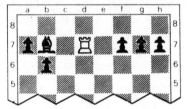

The two white rooks control the
seventh and the black rook has
trapped his own king.
Checkmate!

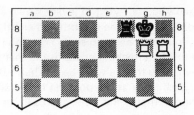

The queen, being more powerful, can make even better use of an open
file than a rook. When she invades the enemy ranks she can threaten mate
in positions where a rook would only give check:

The white queen has invaded the
eighth rank. She also attacks e7
and stops the black king escaping
up the board.

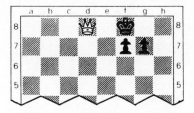

The white queen has seized the
seventh and the black king is
nailed to the edge of the board.

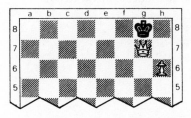

The white queen has again invaded the seventh and the black
king is neatly tied up.

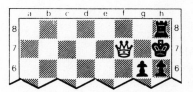

Open files and the enemy ranks

When you are trying to invade down a file in an actual game your biggest problem is that the seventh and eighth ranks are usually heavily guarded by your opponent's pieces. Your job is to get rid of the guards. You can do this by attacking or capturing them, or by deflecting or overloading them. You must always be on the look-out for a sacrifice which removes a guard. Look at the position below and see how Paul Morphy, playing White, removes the three guards in his way.

The black king is shut in the corner. The white rook on e1 has an open file, but Black's queen, rook, and knight heavily defend the back rank against invasion.

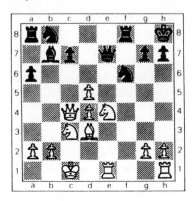

White to move

White captures:

1 Ne4xf6   Qe7xf6

One guard dead...two to go!

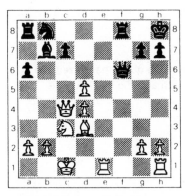

Position after 1 ... Qe7xf6

White attacks:

2 Rh1-f1   Qf6-d8

And captures:

3 Rf1xf8+   Qd8xf8

Two guards dead. . .now only
the queen stands in the way.

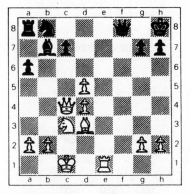

Position after 3 . . . Qd8xf8

White deflects and overloads by
a sacrifice:

4 Qc4-b4   Qf8-c8

Black could not capture; after
4. . . Qf8xb4, 5 Re1-e8 mates.
But now Black's queen has to
defend both the back rank and
the bishop. She can't do both;
she is overloaded.

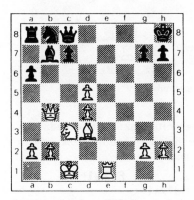

Position after 4 . . . Qf8-c8

White deflects again:

5 Qb4xb7

And White wins. If Black's queen
recaptures she is deflected from
the back rank. If she doesn't recapture Black is a piece down.

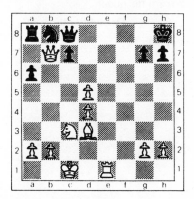

Position after 5 Qb4xb7

TEST THREE

Four problems to solve

Q *How does Black use the open e-file to get a large advantage?*

Q *How can White use the open h-file to force mate in two moves?*

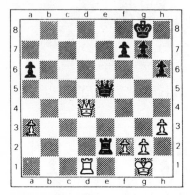

Black to move

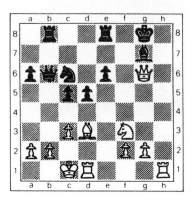

White to move

The white rook is overloaded; he has the queen and the back rank to defend.

1 ...   Re2-e1+
2 Rd1xe1

The white rook has been deflected away from his queen.

2 ...   Qe5xd4

Score 2 points.

The black king is caught by a snap mate:

1 Rh1-h8+   Kg8xh8

Black has no choice.

2 Qg6-h7 mate

Score 3 points.
But *lose 2 points* if you didn't notice Black was threatening 1 . . . Qb6xb2 mate. Don't forget there are two sides to a game.

Q *Black threatens mate. How does White get in first?*

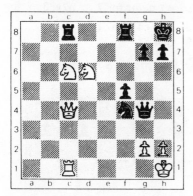

White to move

Q *Again Black threatens mate. Again White can strike first. How?*

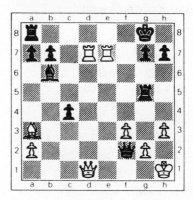

White to move

Black's king is in a coffin. White must get rid of the rooks which guard the back rank. He begins by a clever sacrifice.

1 Qc4-g8+ Kh8xg8

If Black takes with the rook 2 Nd6-f7 is mate.

2 Nc6-e7+ Kg8-h8
3 Nd6-f7+

A second clever sacrifice. White drags one black rook off the back rank. He has already opened the c-file for his own rook to capture and invade at c8.

3 ... Rf8xf7
4 Rc1xc8+ Rf7-f8
5 Rc8xf8 mate

Score 4 points.

White has two targets to attack, the back rank and g7. If he attacks the back rank the black king can escape on f7. If he attacks g7 he has the black rook on g5 to worry about.

1 Qd1-d5+

This queen sacrifice solves both problems. Black has two choices:

(a) **1 . . .Kg8-h8** when the king gets buried alive. (b) **1 . . .Rg5xd5** when the rook is deflected from g7.

(a)
1 ... Kg8-h8
2 Rd7-d8+ Ra8xd8
3 Qd5xd8+ Bb6xd8
4 Re7-e8 mate

Score 3 points if you saw this.

(b)
1 ... Rg5xd5
2 Re7xg7+ Kg8-h8
3 Rg7xh7+ Kh8-g8
4 Rd7-g7 mate

Score 3 more points for this.

Testgame 3

(*Four Knights Opening*)

Paulsen	Morphy
1 e2-e4	e7-e5
2 Ng1-f3	Nb8-c6
3 Nb1-c3	Ng8-f6
4 Bf1-b5	Bf8-c5
5 0-0	0-0
6 Nf3xe5	

If now 6 . . .Nc6xe5, White plays 7 d2-d4 and wins back the piece.

6 ...   **Rf8-e8**

Black plans to win the white e-pawn. His rook will then be well placed on the open file.

7 Ne5xc6

Q *How should Black recapture?*

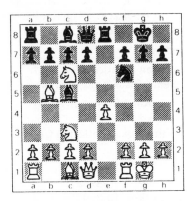

7 ...   **d7xc6**

Score 3 points.
Black keeps all his Q-side pawns in one tidy group, he opens a line for his queen's bishop to come into play, and most important he aims his queen down the d-file and stops

White from putting a pawn firmly in the centre by d2-d4.
Score 1 point for 7 . . .b7xc6.

8 Bb5-c4	b7-b5
9 Bc4-e2	

Q *What should Black do now?*

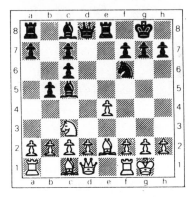

9 ...   **Nf6xe4**

Score 3 points.
If Black doesn't get his pawn back now, he won't get it back at all!

10 Nc3xe4	Re8xe4
11 Be2-f3	

Q *How does Black save his rook?*

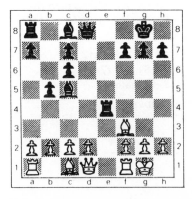

11 . . .   Re4-e6

Score 3 points.

Black has no intention of taking his rook off the open file, and he must defend his pawn on c6.

12 c2-c3

Q *What should Black do now?*

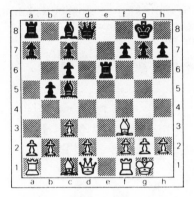

12 . . .   Qd8-d3!

Score 5 points.
Brilliant! Black's move does four things.
First it kills White's plan of setting up a strong pawn centre by 13 d2-d4.
Second by blocking the d-pawn it cramps White and holds up his development.
Third the queen makes way for the other rook to come to e8 and strengthen Black's hold on the open file.
Fourth it hammers at the seventh rank.

If Black can build up enough fire-power on the open e-file he will slash into the heart of White's

position, invade at e1 and e2, and catch the white king in his corner.

Score 2 points if you would have played the sensible developing moves 12 . . .Bc8-b7 or 12 . . .Bc8 -d7; or if you would have strengthened your hold on the open file by 12 . . .Qd8-e7.

13	b2-b4	Bc5-b6
14	a2-a4	b5xa4
15	Qd1xa4	Bc8-d7
16	Ra1-a2	

Q *White wants to play 17 Qa4-c2 and kick the black queen out of d3. What does Black do to stop this plan?*

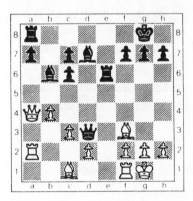

16 . . .   Ra8-e8

Score 4 points.
Black's power down the centre carves White in two. The second black rook adds to the power on the open file, and hits e1 with an immediate threat. 17 Qa4-c2 is answered by 17 . . .Qd3xf1+ 18 Kg1xf1 Re6-e1 mate. White's pieces are powerless on the Q-side.

17 Qa4-a6   Qd3xf3!!

Just as White was beginning to think he was wriggling his way out of trouble, he is belted by a real beauty of a move!

18 g2xf3

If White hadn't captured he would just have been a piece down with a rotten position.

Q *How does Black continue the attack?*

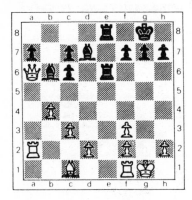

18 ...   Re6-g6+

Score 4 points.

Another file is open, and Black seizes it immediately. Black must keep the pressure on; he must keep White busy. If he relaxes for a moment White's rescue squad will come racing back from the Q-side, and then White's extra queen will tell.

19 Kg1-h1   Bd7-h3

Black threatens 20 ...Bh3-g2+ 21 Kh1-g1 Bg2xf3 and the white king has died on the open file.

20 Rf1-d1

If the rook had gone the other way, the funeral would have taken place on the back rank: 20 Rf1-g1 Rg6xg1+ 21 Kh1xg1 Re8-e1+ etc.

20 ...   Bh3-g2+
21 Kh1-g1   Bg2xf3+
22 Kg1-f1

The white king is becoming a pinball, being knocked from side to side by the black pieces.

Q *What does Black do now?*

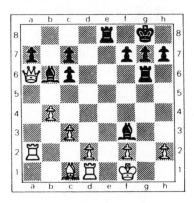

22 ...   Rg6-g2

Score 6 points.

The black rooks hammer down the open files and Black invades the seventh. The black bishops sweep across the diagonals hitting e2, f2, and g2, and White's second rank collapses under the onslaught.

Score 2 points if you would have played 22 ...Bf3xd1.

Score 3 points if you would have played 22 ...Bf3-g2+.

Both these moves keep the attack

alive but give White a chance to organize a defence.
Morphy actually played 22 . . . Bf3-g2+ and although he won comfortably enough, Paulsen was able to hang on into the endgame.

23 Qa6-d3

It was too late for White to fight for the seventh. If 23 d2-d4 Black grabs the back rank by 23 . . . Rg2xh2, and mates on h1.

23 . . . Rg2xf2+

The rook snipes off the sentry pawn and leaves the white king wide open. Stranded, too! The king cannot escape *across* the board, because the rook on e8 has the open file under control. The king cannot escape *up* the board, because the rook on f2 commands the seventh.

24 Kf1-g1

Q *What does Black do now?*

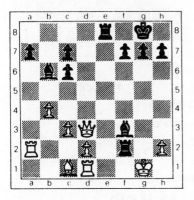

24 . . . Rf2-g2++

Score 4 points.
Black can do more or less what he likes on the seventh rank!

Score 2 points if you would have played 24 . . .Rf2xd2+, which wins but doesn't force checkmate.

Take 5 points off your score if you were going to play 24 . . .Re8-e2. As always the rooks look splendid when doubled on the seventh rank, but you look a bit silly when White plays 25 Qd3-d8+! Don't get too carried away with your own attack and forget about your opponent.

25 Kg1-h1

Q *How does Black end the game?*

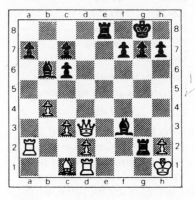

25 . . . Rg2-g1 mate

Score 3 points.
At last a black rook invades the back rank.

Black made fine use of the open e- and g-files. He threatened the back rank and invaded on the seventh. His bishops gave marvellous support as he sniped away at the white defences. The seventh rank fell into his hands, the white king had nowhere to run and was caught in a cross-fire in the corner.

Tartakover bowled over!

Dr Tartakover knew all about open files. He knew how the queen and rooks became more powerful as the pawns were cleared away and the files became open. He knew how to invade the enemy position by attacking the seventh and eighth ranks. Of course he knew. Tartakover was a grandmaster, so he was bound to know. Wasn't he?

Dr Tartakover holds the doubtful honour of being the grandmaster who has been checkmated in the lowest ever number of moves. Eleven! And it all happened because of an open file.

It all began OK:

(Caro-Kann Defence)

Réti	Tartakover
1 e2-e4	c7-c6
2 d2-d4	d7-d5
3 Nb1-c3	d5xe4
4 Nc3xe4	Ng8-f6
5 Qd1-d3	

An unusual move which tempts Tartakover to attack too soon.

5 . . .   **e7-e5?**

Striking back in the centre is the right idea in the Caro–Kann defence, but this is the wrong way of doing it. Tartakover loses far too much time getting back his pawn, while White quietly develops.

6 d4xe5	Qd8-a5+
7 Bc1-d2	Qa5xe5
8 0-0-0!!	

Two open files in the centre! Réti smells blood and sacrifices a piece.

8 . . .   **Nf6xe4**

Tartakover, who obviously hadn't seen what was coming, must have been sitting fairly comfortably at this point. . .

9 Qd3-d8+

. . .it's around here that he probably fell out of his chair!

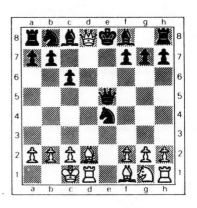

9 . . .	Ke8xd8
10 Bd2-g5++	

Double check!

10 . . .   **Kd8-c7**

Or 10 . . .Kd8-e8 11 Rd1-d8 mate.

11 Bg5-d8 mate

Tartakover certainly knew all about open files after that!

The helpful knight

A rook on the seventh can sometimes be helped by a knight to set
up a standard mating position.

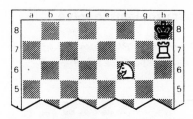

In both of the positions below, White makes clever use of this idea. You
won't score any points, but have a look and see if you can work out what
White does before looking at the answers.

White threatens mate with his rook
on h7 and e8, but both of these
squares are guarded. In one move
White can destroy the guards. How?

In this position White seems to have
no chance of stopping the march
of the black pawns. But the rook
and knight can combine to force
a draw. How?

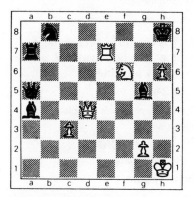

White to move

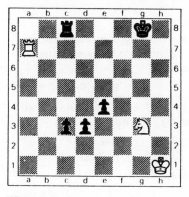

White to move

White plays **1 Qd4-d7**
Brilliant!
If Black captures with the rook he
shuts out his bishop and is mated
on e8. If he takes with the bishop
or knight he shuts out his rook and
is mated on h7. If he doesn't capture
at all, he is mated anyway!

White draws by perpetual check:

1	Ng3xe4	c3-c2
2	Ne4-f6+	Kg8-f8
3	Nf6-h7+	Kf8-e8
4	Nh7-f6+	Ke8-f8

The knight can check all day! If
the black king goes to h8 or d8 he
gets mated by the rook.

TEST FOUR

Four problems to solve

Q *How does Black use the open e-file to get a large advantage?*

Q *How does White use the open d-file to force checkmate?*

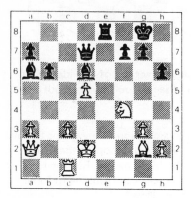

Black to move

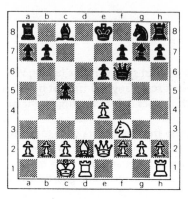

White to move

Black has a good invasion square on e2, but first he must destroy the guard.

1 ...   Bd6xf4+

If White doesn't recapture he will lose his rook as well!

2 g3xf4   Re8-e2+
3 Kd2-d1   Re2xa2

Score 2 points.

Black is behind in development, and the invasion squares d7 and d8 are poorly protected.

1 Bd2-g5

The black queen is attacked and driven away.

1 ...   Qf6-g6
2 Rd1-d8 mate

Score 3 points.

Q *White seems to be pressing forward with his queen and rook, but it is Black who can force checkmate. How?*

Q *White's heavy pieces command the open files and he has invasion points on the seventh and eighth ranks. How does he force checkmate?*

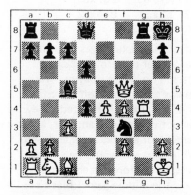

Black to move

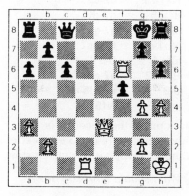

White to move

The black knight is the key to the problem. On f3 it is in position to set up a standard mate.

1 ...   Qd8-h4

2 Rg4-g2

Or 2 Rg4xh4 Rg8-g1 mate.

2 ...   Qh4xh2+

3 Rg2xh2   Rg8-g1 mate

Score 4 points.

White can see a standard mating position, but first he must deflect the black queen.

1 Rd1-d8+   Qc8xd8

2 Qe3-e6+   Kg8-h7

3 Rf6xh6+   g7xh6

4 Qe6-f7 mate

Score 6 points.

Testgame 4

(*Benoni Defence*)

	Capablanca	Mieses
1	d2-d4	Ng8-f6
2	Ng1-f3	c7-c5
3	d4-d5	d7-d6
4	c2-c4	g7-g6
5	Nb1-c3	Bf8-g7
6	e2-e4	0-0
7	Bf1-e2	e7-e6
8	0-0	e6xd5
9	e4xd5	Nf6-e8

Black opens the diagonal for his bishop to capture on c3 and scatter White's pawns, but this plan is slow.

Q *What should White do now?*

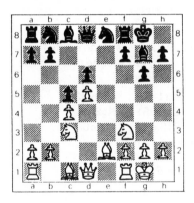

10 Rf1-e1

Score 4 points.
White must carry on with the job of developing his pieces; so the rook takes up a good post on an open file.

Score 2 points for 10 Bc1-g5 or 10 Bc1-f4. Both of these are sensible

developing moves, but it isn't yet clear which will be the better square for the bishop, so it makes more sense to develop the rook first.

10	...	Bc8-g4
11	Nf3-g5	Bg7xc3
12	b2xc3	Bg4xe2
13	Qd1xe2	

After these exchanges the game has a clear pattern. Black has messed up White's pawns. The pawns are doubled on the c-file, and the a-pawn is isolated. They cannot defend one another, and are targets for attack. In an endgame White's pawns would be a weakness, but before the endgame we have the middle-game! Black's plan has been slow and White has three advantages which will give him a quick middle-game attack. He has better development, he has more space, and he has seized the open e-file with an immediate invasion point on e7.

13 ... Ne8-g7

Q *What does White do now?*

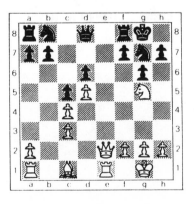

14 Ng5-e4

Score 4 points.
The knight hits two important
squares, d6 and f6. It prevents
Black from fighting for the open
file because 14 . . .Rf8-e8 can be
answered by 15 Bc1-g5 and 16
Ne4-f6+.

Score 1 point for 14 Bc1-f4 or 14
Ra1-b1.

14 . . .   f7-f6

Black shuts the bishop out of g5,
but hands White another invasion
point, e6, on the open file.

Q *What should White do now?*

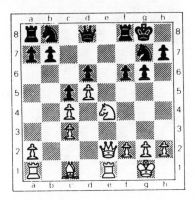

15 Bc1-f4

Score 4 points.
Good development with a threat.
Black must now take time off from
his own development to defend his
d-pawn.

Score 2 points for 15 Bc1-h6.
Score 1 point for 15 Ra1-b1.

15 . . .   Ng7-e8
16 Bf4-h6   Ne8-g7

White has cleverly gained a move.

Black couldn't play 16 . . .Rf8-f7
because he would have lost control of e8 and been flattened down
the open file after 17 Ne4-g5.

Q *How does White continue
the attack?*

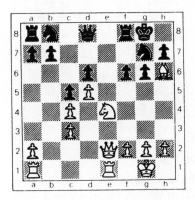

17 Ra1-d1

Score 3 points.
The rook is to be brought over to
the K-side. White is getting ready
to plant a major piece on e7. He
will then snipe sideways along the
seventh rank at f7, g7, and h7; so
his other pieces must be in position
to finish off the attack.

Score 1 point for 17 Ra1-b1.
The b-file is not much use to the
white rook because Black can
block any chance of an invasion
just by putting a pawn on b6.

17 . . .   Nb8-a6
18 Rd1-d3   f6-f5
19 Ne4-g5

Now e6 comes under fire. White
threatens 20 Bh6xg7 Kg8xg7
21 Ng5-e6+.

19 ...   Na6-c7

Q *What is White's next move?*

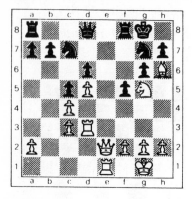

20 Qe2-e7!

Score 5 points.
All of White's pieces are well placed; so the invasion begins on the open file.

20 ...   Qd8xe7
21 Re1xe7

Even with the queens gone the attack sails on, and the seventh rank becomes the battlefield.

21 ...   Nc7-e8

Q *What does White do now?*

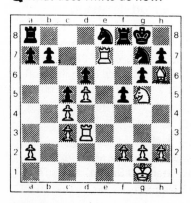

22 Rd3-h3

Score 4 points.
White is hammering mercilessly at the door, f7, g7, and h7. The wood is splintering, and when White crashes in the black king will be trapped in his death cell.

Score 1 point for 22 Re7xb7. This can't be bad, but winning kings is better than winning pawns . . .and more fun!

22 ...   f5-f4
23 Bh6xg7   Ne8xg7

Q *What does White play now?*

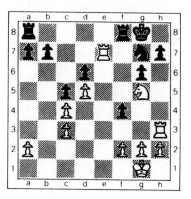

24 Rh3xh7

Score 3 points.
The two rooks join forces on the seventh, the cell door has collapsed, and there is an immediate threat of 25 Re7xg7 mate.
You score nothing for 24 Ng5xh7 or 24 Re7xb7 which allow Black to fight back on the open files.

24 ...   Ng7-f5

Q *What does White play now?*

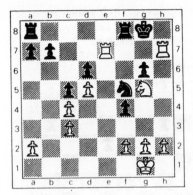

25 Re7-e6!

Score 5 points.

As long as the black knight defends g7 the rooks can't force mate on the seventh rank; so White uses the open file to snipe at a new target, g6.

Score 1 point for 25 Re7xb7, which still wins a pawn, but gives Black the time to work up a counter-attack. If Black can get a rook working on the open e-file he will have the chance to fight back, so White must keep up the pressure, he must keep Black busy defending against threats.

Take 4 points off your score if you didn't notice your rook was attacked, and did something else.

25 ... Rf8-e8

Black makes a final bid to fight for the open file, but he only gets himself mated!

26 Re6xg6+ Nf5-g7

There's nothing Black can do except wait and get mated. In the actual game Mieses didn't even bother to wait; he resigned!

Q *What does White do now?*

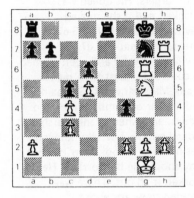

27 Rh7xg7+

Score 3 points.

The only way to force mate. If White captures with the other rook he still has a winning position, but the two rooks cannot force mate on the seventh rank. Now, whichever way the black king runs he will be mated by either 28 Rg7-h7 or 28 Rg7-f7.

White used the open file as an invasion route. With his rook firmly entrenched on e7 he switched the point of attack to the squares on the seventh rank in front of the enemy king. With the seventh rank under his command he returned to the open file and used e6 as the springboard for his mating attack.

How Levitzky lost...and won?

Levitzky stared at the board thoughtfully. Opposite him Marshall was considering his next move; he looked happy, too happy Levitzky thought. Levitzky was a piece down, but his position wasn't that bad.

Marshall's rook and knight were both targets. His queen was attacked and if she moved Levitzky could play Rc5-c7, threatening mate on g7. Levitzky's queen and rook seemed to control the best files, but... Frank Marshall was U.S. Champion, and master of combinations and tactics, and when Frank Marshall looked happy, Levitzky knew it was his turn to look worried! But why should he be worried? He'd worked it all out. There was nothing to worry about ...

Marshall to move

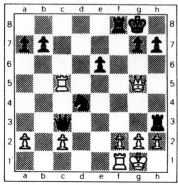

Levitzky

That was when Levitzky got his shock. Marshall moved. Marshall made a move that has been described as the greatest move ever played. Marshall played **1 ...Qc3-g3!!** Levitzky, when he had picked himself up from the floor, resigned.

Marshall threatens mate on the seventh, 2 ...Qg3xh2.

If Levitzky captures with a pawn, he opens a file and gets mated:
(a) 2 h2xg3 Nd4-e2 mate.
(b) 2 f2xg3 Nd4-e2+ 3 Kg1-h1 Rf8xf1 mate.

If Levitzky captures with his queen he gets forked: 2 Qg5xg3 Nd4-e2+ 3 Kg1-h1 Ne2xg3+, and he comes out a piece down.

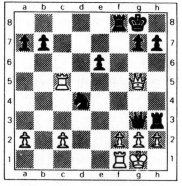

Position after 1 ...Qc3-g3!!

Brilliant! The spectators at the tournament in Breslau in 1912 thought so. They showered the board with gold coins — so perhaps Levitzky got something out of the game after all!

The dance of the king

White is winning.

Well, it's obvious isn't it?

He's got seven pawns more, and he only has to get his rook on to the open a-file, or on to the back rank at d8, and Black will be mated. But it is Black's move, and Black plays:

1 ...   Rf8-f3+

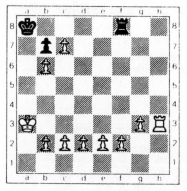

Black to move

Very clever. If White captures, 2 e2xf3, Black is stalemated and escapes with a draw. If White moves his king, Black just checks again with his rook. If White puts a pawn in the way, Black just takes it. If White takes the rook it is stalemate, if he doesn't he cannot avoid perpetual check. So the game is drawn. Or is it?

White wins by getting checkmate on the open a-file:

2 e2-e3   Rf3xe3+
3 c2-c3   Re3xc3+
4 Ka3-a2   Rc3-a3+
5 Ka2-b1   Ra3-a1+
6 Kb1-c2   Ra1-c1+

The king leads a merry dance in and out of the pawns. The rook has no choice; he must follow.

7 Kc2-d3   Rc1-c3+
8 Kd3-e2   Rc3-e3+
9 Ke2-f1   Re3-e1+
10 Kf1-g2   Re1-g1+
11 Kg2-f3   Rg1xg3+
12 Kf3-e2

Back we go! But now the White Rook can come to a3! And Black hasn't time for 12 ... Rg3xh3 because of 13 c7-c8=Q mate.

12 ...   Rg3-e3+
13 Ke2-d1   Re3-e1+
14 Kd1-c2   Re1-c1+
15 Kc2-b3   Rc1-c3+
16 Kb3-a2   Rc3-a3+
17 Rh3xa3   checkmate!

TEST FIVE

Four problems to solve

Q *It is Black's move. Is it safe for his rook to capture the white pawn on d5?*

Q *White threatens to capture on h6 and mate. How does Black use the g-file and seventh rank to strike first?*

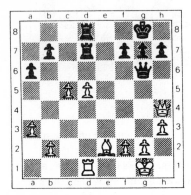

Black to move

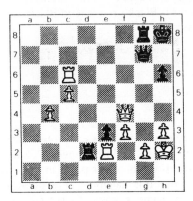

Black to move

No! Black does not have enough control of his first rank.

1 ...	Rd7xd5
2 Qh4xd8+	

The white queen is sacrificed to force the invasion.

2 ...	Rd5xd8
3 Rd1xd8 mate	

Score 2 points.

The invasion square is g2 and White doesn't have enough defenders.

1 ...	Qg7xg2+
2 Re2xg2	Rd2xg2+

Not 2 ...Rg8xg2+ when the white king escapes.

3 Kh2-h1	Rg2-g1+
4 Kh1-h2	Rg8-g2 mate

Score 3 points.

Q *How does White force checkmate?*

Q *White will have to give up a rook to avoid mate. How does Black win?*

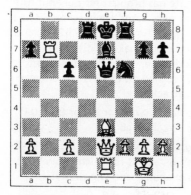

White to move

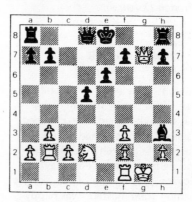

Black to move

Black's king looks completely safe surrounded by all his own pieces. In fact Black's pieces only get in the way!

1 Be3-c5

White's strength is on the open e-file and along the seventh rank. The two lines meet at e7; so this point becomes the target.

1 ...   Qe6xe2

If 1 . . .Be7xc5 he loses his queen.

2 Rb7xe7+   Qe2xe7
3 Re1xe7 mate

Black's king has been stabbed between his own guards.

Score 4 points.

Black has a standard mate on the open g-file, but he must first deflect the white queen.

1 ...   Qd8-f6
2 Qg7xf6

If White retreats his queen along the g-file he leaves his rooks to be taken.

2 ...   Rh8-g8+
3 Kg1-h1   Bh3-g2+
4 Kh1-g1   Bg2xf3+

. . .and Black mates next move.

Score 6 points.

Testgame 5

(*French Defence*)

Kovacs   Korchnoi

1 e2-e4	e7-e6
2 d2-d4	d7-d5
3 e4xd5	e6xd5

Straight away we have an open file. Open files can be used in many ways. Maybe when he exchanged pawns Kovacs planned to use the open e-file to exchange the rooks and perhaps the queens. Maybe Kovacs, playing one of the world's leading grandmasters, was happy to head for a draw. Korchnoi had other plans for the open file. Korchnoi decided to bash Kovacs flat!

4 Bf1-d3	Nb8-c6
5 c2-c3	Bf8-d6
6 Qd1-f3	Nc6-e7
7 Bc1-f4	Ng8-f6
8 h2-h3	

White stops 8 . . . Bc8-g4.

Q *What should Black do now?*

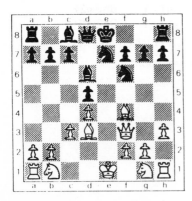

8 . . .   **Bd6xf4**

Score 3 points.

White has brought his queen into play very early. He has already had to waste time playing 8 h2-h3, and now Black makes White lose even more time. The white queen is to be dragged on to f4 where she can be attacked.

Score 2 points for either 8 . . . 0-0 or 8 . . . Ne7-g6.

Lose 2 points for both 8 . . . Ne7-f5 and 8 . . . Bc8-f5 which allow White to exchange and win material.

9 Qf3xf4	0-0
10 Ng1-e2	Ne7-g6
11 Qf4-h2	

Q *What should Black do now?*

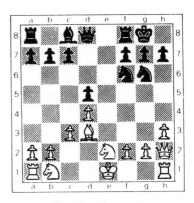

11 . . .   **Rf8-e8**

Score 2 points.

If Black is to make use of the open file he has to grab control quickly. White must not be allowed to complete his development quietly and put a rook on e1.

Even so, Korchnoi did not play the best move:

Score 3 points for 11 . . .Qd8-e7; you will see why in a minute!

12   0-0

Q*What should Black do now?*

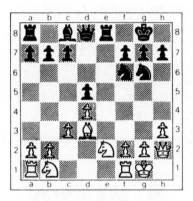

12 . . .   Bc8-f5!

Score 4 points.

Black brings his last minor piece into play and smashes his way on to the seventh rank.

Score 1 point for 12 . . .Qd8-e7 or 12 . . .Nf6-e4.

13   Bd3xf5

The white bishop is deflected and leaves his second rank unguarded.

13 . . .   Re8xe2

Black invades, but now we see why . . . Qd8-e7 would have been better on move 11. If the invasion of the seventh had been carried out by the black queen, White would have been in real trouble.

14   b2-b3

Q*How does Black continue the build-up?*

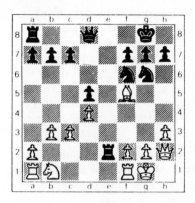

14 . . .   Qd8-e7

Score 3 points.

Good development. The queen adds her power to the rook on the open file, and she hits a3 stopping White from developing his knight.

15   Bf5-d3   Re2-b2

Having seized the seventh rank, Black isn't going to let go.

16   Qh2-g3

Q*What does Black do now?*

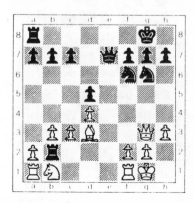

16 ...   Ra8-e8

Score 3 points.

Black completes his development, and his pieces make a fine sight. A rook is established on the seventh rank, the open e-file is under control, and the knights are ready to pounce. If you haven't yet noticed that the rook on b2 is about to be trapped don't worry...Korchnoi didn't notice it either!

Score 3 points for 16 ...a7-a5 which saves the rook and threatens to open a new line of attack.

17 Qg3-g5   Nf6-e4!

The knight moves in to hit out at the seventh.

18 Qg5-c1

White traps the black rook, but Black's pieces are so well placed that he finds a good answer.

18 ...   Rb2xf2!
19 Rf1xf2   Ne4xf2
20 Kg1xf2

Q *How does Black continue the attack?*

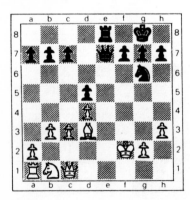

20 ...   Qe7-f6+

Score 3 points.

White has picked up a piece, but his army, huddled together on the Q-side, seems to have deserted its king. Black has two good files, and invasion points at e2 and f2. Korchnoi begins the bashing!

Score 2 points for 20 ...Qe7-h4+.

21 Kf2-g1   Ng6-f4

With one move Black hits four targets, the bishop, the sentry pawns, and the invasion point e2.

22 Bd3-f1

Q *What is Black's next attacking move?*

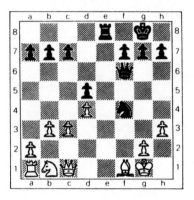

22 ...   Re8-e2!!

Score 5 points.

For the second time a black rook uses the open file to invade the seventh. If the bishop captures, Black retakes with the knight and forks White's king and queen.

Score 2 points for 22 ...Qf6-g5 which threatens to win the queen by 23 ...Nf4xh3+.

23 Nb1-d2

Q *What does Black do now?*

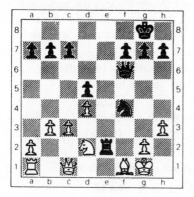

23 ... Nf4xh3+!

Score 4 points.
A rook is firmly planted on the seventh rank, the queen is breathing fire down the f-file; their paths cross at f2, the new invasion target. If White captures the knight his whole second rank collapses: 24 g2xh3 Qf6-f2+ 25 Kg1-h1 Qf2-h2 mate.

24 Kg1-h2 Nh3-f4
25 Kh2-g3

Q *What does Black do now?*

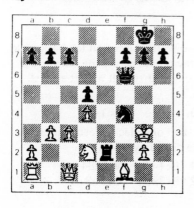

25 ... Nf4-d3

Score 3 points.
The white queen is attacked and the knight makes way for his lady to come to f4 or f2. Kovacs had had enough of the bashing at this point and resigned. We shall play on for a couple of moves to see how Korchnoi would have finished him off.

26 Qc1-d1

A last attempt at getting rid of the black rook.

Q *How does Black force mate?*

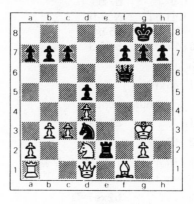

26 ... Qf6-f4+
27 Kg3-h3 Nd3-f2 mate

Score 4 points.
A most suitable finish! Black's rook and queen still sit upon their open files. White has failed to kick the rook out of the invasion square e2. Black has given mate from his other invasion square, f2, not with a major piece, but with a knight.

Tramp, tramp, tramp, the pawns are marching

This is a club game between two Australians. White invades the back rank and tries to batter his way along it to get at the black king. He grinds to a halt at the gatehouse to the fortress. That's when he decides to send for the reinforcements!

(*Sicilian Defence*)

	Sumpter	King
1	e2-e4	c7-c5
2	Ng1-f3	Nb8-c6
3	d2-d4	c5xd4
4	Nf3xd4	e7-e6
5	Nb1-c3	Qd8-c7
6	Bf1-e2	a7-a6
7	0-0	b7-b5
8	Kg1-h1	Ng8-f6
9	f2-f4	b5-b4
10	e4-e5	b4xc3

Chop. . .

| 11 | e5xf6 | |

. . . and counter chop!

| 11 | . . . | c3xb2 |
| 12 | f6xg7 | |

The foot soldiers hack their way merrily to promotion.

| 12 | . . . | b2xa1=Q |
| 13 | g7xh8=Q | |

A white queen appears on the back rank. She peers at the black king, snug in his fortress. The black bishop on f8 represents the gate-house, portcullis, and about three feet of oak door. The queen rams the door, but it doesn't budge. Clearly she needs help. . .reinforcements!

13	. . .	Qa1xa2
14	Qh8xh7	a6-a5
15	h2-h4	

Help is on its way! Another foot soldier strides forward.

15	. . .	a5-a4
16	h4-h5	a4-a3
17	h5-h6	Qa2-b1
18	Qh7-g8	

Get out of the way ladies!

18	. . .	a3-a2
19	h6-h7	a2-a1=Q
20	h7-h8=Q	

Two white queens on the back rank! They pound across the drawbridge and hurl their full weight against f8. . .

| 20 | . . . | Qb1-b4 |

. . .and one black queen makes sure the door stays shut.

| 21 | Bc1-e3 | Nc6xd4 |
| 22 | Be3xd4 | Qa1-a3 |

If White's female battering ram could not smash its way past f8 before this move, it has little chance now.

23 Be2-h5

Unable to batter his way in at the front door White nips round to the side entrance, f7.

23 ... d7-d5

Another black queen comes to the rescue. White has a problem. Even with two queens on the back rank he cannot find a way to flatten Black's defences. Clearly the attackers need help. . .reinforcements!

24 f4-f5

Inspired by the daring deeds of his comrades, private f-pawn takes to the warpath. Barrel of gunpowder in one arm, match and fuse in the other, he marches to glory.

24 ... Bc8-a6

Black's e-pawn could have clumped private f-pawn on the head and ended all his dreams of honour and glory. But 24 . . . e6xf5 would have opened the e-file at the end of which White has a good target to attack — the black king.

25 f5xe6 0-0-0

The black king realizes his side door is about to be kicked in, and takes refuge behind his rook.

26 Rf1xf7

Attacked by queen, rook, and bishop, not to mention private f-pawn and barrel of gunpowder, f7 finally crumbles under the barrage.

26 ... Qc7-a5
27 c2-c3 Qb4-d6

Black grimly props up his gate-house.

28 Bh5-g4

Two queens on the eighth, a rook on the seventh, and White still can't get past f8.

28 ... Rd8-e8?

Black has spent so long guarding his front door that he's forgotten it's moveable! He should have played 28 . . .Bf8-e7 and left the white queens waving their battering ram at thin air.

29 e6-e7+

Gunpowder in position. . .fuse ready. . .private f-pawn strikes the match. . .

29 ... Kc8-b8
30 e7xf8=Q

. . .and blows the gatehouse sky high! The defences in ruins, the white queens can pour into the Black position; so Black decides the time has come to haul up the white flag.

30 ... Black resigns

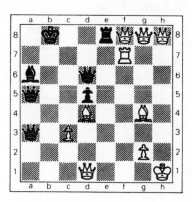

TEST SIX

Four problems to solve

Q *How does White use the seventh rank to force checkmate?*

Q *How does Black invade the back rank and force checkmate?*

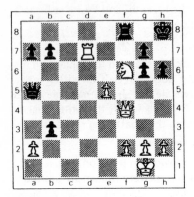

White to move

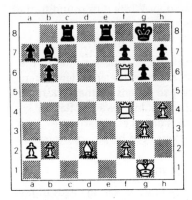

Black to move

White has to get rid of the black g-pawn to force a standard rook-and-knight mate.

1 Qf4xh6+   g7xh6

Now the seventh rank is clear.

2 Rd7-h7 mate

Score 2 points.

Lose 1 point if you didn't notice Black was threatening 1 . . .Qa5-e1 mate.

The white bishop is overloaded; he has to guard both of the invasion squares, c1 and e1.

1 . . .   Rc8-c1+
2 Bd2xc1

The bishop has been deflected away from e1.

2 . . .   Re8-e1+
3 Kg1-h2   Re1-h1 mate

Score 3 points.

Q *How does Black make use of the centre files?*

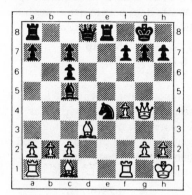

Black to move

White is behind in development, and his first rank is not properly defended. Black forces his way to the back line.

| 1 ... | Qd8xd3 |
| 2 c2xd3 | Ne4-f2+ |

And now White must give up his queen, since 3 Rf1xf2 leaves the back rank undefended and 3 . . . Re8-e1 mates.

| 3 Kh1-g1 | Nf2xg4+ |

. . .and Black has come out a piece to the good.

Score 5 points.

Q *How does Black use his two open files?*

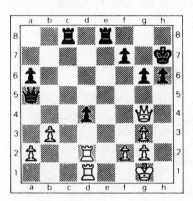

Black to move

The white pieces imprison their own king. Black has to force entry for his rooks on to the back line.

1 ...	Qa5xd2
2 Rd1xd2	Re8-e1+
3 Kg1-h2	Rc8-c1

. . . and White can avoid mate on h1 only by giving up both queen and rook.

| 4 Rd2-d1 | Rc1xd1 |
| 5 Qg4xd1 | Re1xd1 |

Score 5 points.

Testgame 6

(*Danish Gambit*)

Charousek	Wollner
1 e2-e4	e7-e5
2 d2-d4	e5xd4
3 Ng1-f3	Bf8-c5
4 c2-c3	d4xc3
5 Nb1xc3	d7-d6

This is a normal gambit position. Black has an extra pawn and hopes to make it count in an endgame. White has a pawn in the centre, more space, and a lead in development, all of which he hopes will help him to work up a sharp attack.

Q *How should White continue his development?*

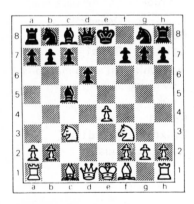

6 Bf1-c4

Score 3 points.
Sensible development. White puts his bishop on a good diagonal aiming at the weak point f7, and prepares to castle.

Score 1 point for 6 Bc1-g5 or 6 Bc1-f4. It isn't clear yet which will be the best square for this bishop; so White does best to get on with the moves he knows he must play.

6 ...	Ng8-f6
7 0-0	0-0
8 Nf3-g5?	

A strange move, moving the knight a second time when other pieces are waiting to be developed. Black should now have played 8 . . . Nb8-c6 when he would have had a fine position. However. . .

8 ...	h7-h6
9 Ng5xf7	Rf8xf7

Q *How does White continue the attack?*

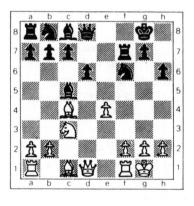

10 e4-e5!

Score 5 points.
A strong move based on White's power on the d-file. Black cannot capture the pawn because if he opens the d-file he loses his queen.

Score 2 points for 10 Bc4xf7+.

10 ...   Nf6-g4

Q *What should White do now?*

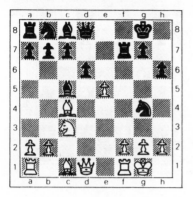

11 e5-e6

Score 4 points.
White threatens 12 e6xf7+ and
12 Qd1xg4.

Black seems to be in a good position
to use the open f-file, but if he tries
to do so it rebounds upon him: 11
...Rf7xf2 12 e6-e7+ Rf2-f7+
13 Kg1-h1, and it is the white rook
that is firing down the file.

11 ...   Qd8-h4

Q *What is White's next move?*

12 e6xf7+

Score 2 points.
The rook can be taken for nothing,
and with check! At the same time
the e-file is opened and the pawn
attacks e8, which will be an excellent invasion square.

12 ...   Kg8-f8

Q *What should White do now?*

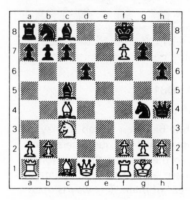

13 Bc1-f4

Score 3 points.
White defends against the mate
threat on h2, develops a piece, and
prepares to bring his queen's rook
on to the open e-file.

Score 1 point for 13 h2-h3.
Lose 5 points if you didn't notice
Black was threatening 13 . . .Qh4xh2
mate.

13 ...   Ng4xf2

This is the only way for Black to
keep his attack going, but with
three of his pieces at home in bed
on the Q-side he hasn't much chance
of success. All Black does is open the
f-file for the white rook!

Q How does White save his queen?　**Q** What does White do now?

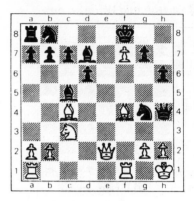

14　Qd1-e2

Score 2 points.

White has been forced to play a good move! His queen seizes the open file and hits the invasion square, e8, with an immediate threat of mate. The way is open for a white rook to add its power along the e-file: e8 is going to be hammered hard!

Lose 3 points if you were going to play 14 Qd1-e1 when you lose your queen after 14 . . . Nf2-d3 discovering check.

Lose 3 points for 14 Qd1-d2 which also loses the queen, to 14 . . . Nf2-e4+.

14　. . .　Nf2-g4+
15　Kg1-h1　Bc8-d7

Black defends e8 and makes a last desperate attempt to bring his Q-side pieces into the game.

16　Ra1-e1

Score 4 points.

Naturally the rook comes to the open file, and mate is threatened on e8 once again. There is no way Black can fight for the file; so it is just a matter of White hammering away until he can force the invasion.

16　. . .　Nb8-c6

Q How does White invade the black position?

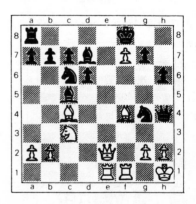

17 Qe2-e8+!!

Score 6 points.
Black seems to have the invasion square safely guarded, but White smashes down the file with a queen sacrifice.

Score 2 points for 17 Bc4-e6, trying to exchange the black bishop.

Score 2 points for 17 Qe2-e4, trying to sneak onto the eighth rank through the back door on h7.

Score 2 points for 17 Nc3-d5.

17 ... Ra8xe8

Q *How should White recapture?*

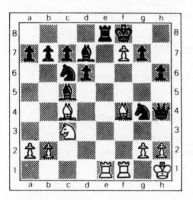

18 f7xe8=Q+!

Score 3 points.
A second queen sacrifice: the right way to keep the attack going.

18 ... Bd7xe8

White has sacrificed a second queen, but now he has the open f-file as a second invasion route.

Q *What does White do now?*

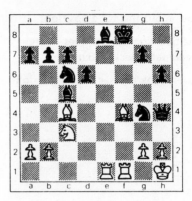

19 Bf4xd6 mate

Score 3 points.
The double check brings the game to a sudden end.

Black accepted a pawn in the opening but he fell behind in development. He fell further behind when he played 8 . . .h7-h6. White won a lot of space for his pieces and worked up a sharp attack. When Black tried to fight back he only succeeded in opening first the e-file and then the f-file for White's major pieces. Black hurriedly tried to race his Q-side pieces out to defend the invasion squares, but he was too late, and White's brilliant double queen sacrifice killed him off.

The pawn pincher pays the penalty

How about this for a position!

The question is, how does White checkmate Black in 8 moves?

Have a look and see if you can do it.

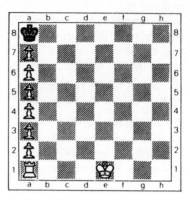

White to move

The key, as you have probably guessed, is the open file.
But which open file?
The a-file!
But the a-file isn't open! In fact it's the only file that isn't open.
No, but that's the point.
Black is going to be invited to open it by taking all the white pawns.

1 0-0-0

The white king takes up position for the checkmate. . .

1 . . .   Ka8xa7

. . .and the black king is forced to begin his march to the scaffold.

2 Rd1-d8   Ka7xa6

No choice!

3 Rd8-d7   Ka6xa5

On. . .

4 Rd7-d6   Ka5xa4

. . .and on. . .

5 Rd6-d5   Ka4xa3

. . .he goes. . .

6 Rd5-d4   Ka3xa2

. . .until there are no pawns left. . .

7 Rd4-d3   Ka2-a1

. . .and White mates on the file Black has so kindly opened!

8 Rd3-a3 mate

Neat!

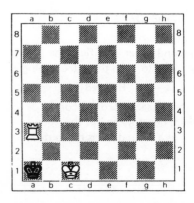

The queen who climbed a mountain...and fell off!

In which the white queen climbs the mountain, slowly, step by step, scrabbling for foothold, clawing the rock. At last the summit is in sight. The queen plants her flag on h8, the bells ring, the people cheer. Proud and majestic, she waves to the crowds. Her moment of glory. Then, disaster seems to strike. She totters, grasps out at thin air . . . and falls. Pride and majesty gone she plummets screaming to the depths below, crown toppling, skirts swirling. The crowd stand stunned, speechless — but all is well. A sharp tug at the ripcord, her parachute billows out, and she slides gracefully down to a perfect two-point landing. Dignity and control restored, she turns, and blasts the black king with a blockbuster of a broadside.

Well, here's our white queen at the foot of the mountain.

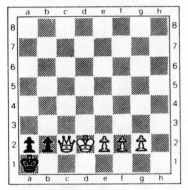

White to move

If she checks on d1, Black simply queens his pawn and escapes with a draw. So...

1 Qc2-c3

...the queen begins her climb.

1 ...   **Ka1-b1**

The black king finds his b-pawn can't move; he sticks out his nose to find out why...

2 Qc3-d3+

...and gets ordered back home.

2 ...   **Kb1-a1**
3 Qd3-d4

One step higher.

3 ...   **Ka1-b1**

The king has another look . . . after all there isn't anything else to do!

4 Qd4-e4+   **Kb1-a1**
5 Qe4-e5   **Ka1-b1**
6 Qe5-f5+   **Kb1-a1**
7 Qf5-f6

Up, up she goes!

7 ...   **Ka1-b1**
8 Qf6-g6+   **Kb1-a1**
9 Qg6-g7

High into the snow and ice.

9 ...   **Ka1-b1**
10 Qg7-h7+   **Kb1-a1**
11 Qh7-h8

The queen completes her zig-zag path to the top. . .

11 ...   **Ka1-b1**

...and dives down the file to kill on the rank. . .

12 Qh8-h1 mate

How to win a rook in six simple steps

Black has just played . . .Rb8xb2, gobbling up a white pawn. He thinks everything is safely guarded, but. . .

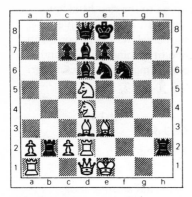

White to move

. . .White wins the rook because of the open d-file and castling!

1 Nd4xe6

Step one. White threatens both the queen and 2 Bd3-g6 mate, so Black doesn't have time for anything clever.

1 . . .   Bd7xe6
2 Nd5xf6+

Step two. Black is in check and must recapture.

2 . . .   e7xf6
3 Rd2xh2

Step three. Gradually the smoke is cleared from the d-file.

3 . . .   Bd6xh2
4 Bd3-g6+

Step four. The black king is tied to his queen.

4 . . .   Ke8-e7
5 Qd1xd8+

Step five. The file is cleared of all remaining rubbish.

5 . . .   Ke7xd8
6 0-0-0+

Step six. The black rook pays for his greed.

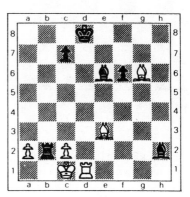

Diagonals and bishops

Bishops, like rooks, need open lines if they are to work at full power. And equally important to a bishop is the position of the pawns.
In the diagram below there are three points to consider:

(1) The white bishop operates on the dark squares.

(2) The white pawns all stand on dark squares. They are fixed and have no hope of moving forward.

(3) The black pawns are all on light squares. They can't be attacked.

The bishop is useless because his own pawns get in his way and he can't get at his opponent's pawns.

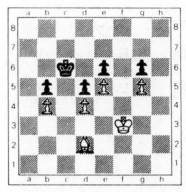

A draw — White can't break through.

In this diagram the position has changed and the bishop is powerful.

(1) The white bishop operates on the light squares.

(2) The white pawns all stand on dark squares. They don't get in the way of the bishop.

(3) The black pawns are all on light squares. They can be attacked!

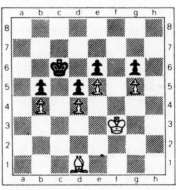

White wins!

Both of these positions are endgames with just the kings, bishop, and pawns on the board. This makes it easier to see the power of the bishop, but it would be just the same in a middle-game position. The bishop would be just as good, or bad, if there were other pieces on the board.

Diagonals and bishops

Straight away we can make some general rules:

(a) *Your bishop will lose power if your own pawns are fixed on squares of the same colour.*

(b) *Your two bishops will work best if your pawns are equally balanced between light and dark squares.*

Now look at the bishop in this position:

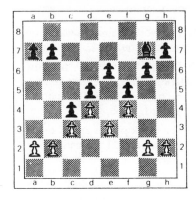

(1) The black bishop operates on dark squares.
(2) Black's pawns do not get in the way of his bishop.
(3) The pawn position is blocked.
(4) The white pawns form a barrier, a blockade to the bishop.

The bishop is a poor piece. It cannot move freely about the board and it has no obvious targets to attack.

This gives us two more rules:

(c) *Your bishop will lose power if the pawn position is blocked.*

(d) *You can use your pawns to set up a blockade and deaden the power of an enemy bishop.*

The two important tactical strengths of a bishop are the skewer and the pin.

The skewer
In a skewer a bishop nails two enemy pieces together on a diagonal. The first piece is forced to move, leaving the second to be captured.

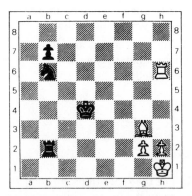

White wins this position by a simple skewer.

White to move

The important diagonal is from g1 to a7.

White plays:

1 Rh6xb6   Rb2xb6

Now the two black pieces are on that diagonal.

2 Bg3-f2+

The black king must leave the diagonal, and then the rook can be captured.

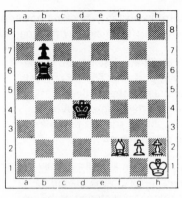

King and rook skewered!

The pin

In a pin a bishop nails one enemy piece to a more valuable enemy piece on the same diagonal.

White wins this position by making use of a simple pin.

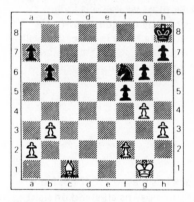

White to move

The important diagonal is from a1 to h8.

White plays:

1 Bc1-b2

Now the knight is pinned: nailed firmly to his king.

1 . . .   Kh8-g7
2 g4-g5

The black knight is attacked again and it cannot move.

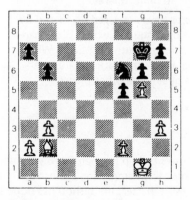

Knight, pinned and lost!

A third important attacking power of a bishop is its ability to weaken the enemy king's position by making 'holes' in the castle wall.

The black king seems safe in the castled position. The three black pawns act as the castle wall, shielding their king. They also attack all the squares on rank 6 in front of them.

White's queen and bishop have joined forces on the diagonal, and mate is threatened on h7.

Black must weaken his king position by moving a pawn. He must make holes in his castle wall.

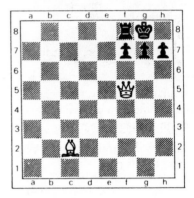

Black to move

Black has played . . .g7-g6. Now his three pawns all stand on light squares; so they only attack and defend light squares.

Holes have appeared on f6 and h6, the dark squares which Black cannot defend with his pawns. White can attack the dark squares with his queen and other pieces.

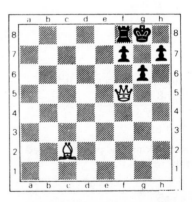

White's bishop has helped to weaken the Black king's position. The bishop is now left hammering against the blockade of light-squared pawns. This doesn't matter; the bishop has done a vital job, and he may still be able to help in the attack.

The bishop helped the queen and rook force checkmate in several of the positions we looked at in the section on open files.
Here are three more mating positions where the bishop lends a hand.

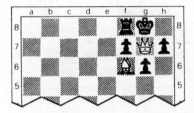

One bishop on his own can't often force checkmate, but here is a position where he can make a real nuisance of himself!

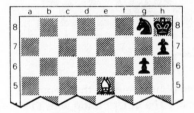

Two bishops side by side are always dangerous raking across the board. Here they prove a deadly weapon.

Here the bishops catch the king in a cross-fire.

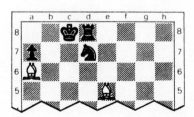

TEST SEVEN

Four problems to solve

Q *Black has two good bishops. How can he make use of them to score a quick victory?*

Q *The white bishops rake the black K-side. How do they help White to force checkmate?*

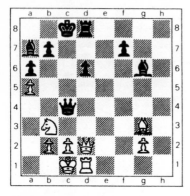

Black to move

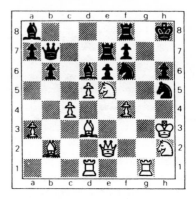

White to move

One bishop helps to threaten mate on c2. The other bishop wins the game with a deadly pin.

1 ...   Ba7-e3

The white queen is pinned and attacked.

2 Qd2xe3   Qc4xc2 mate

Score 2 points.

White must clear the line of action for his bishop on b2 to join the attack.

1 Qe2xh5

Threatening to capture on h6 and mate on h7.

1 ...   Nf6xh5

2 Ne5xf7 mate

Double check!

Score 3 points.

Q *White's pieces are well placed for a king attack. How does he force checkmate?*

Q *The white king is neatly parcelled up. But how can Black get at him?*

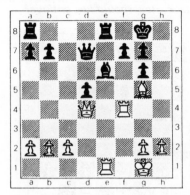

White to move

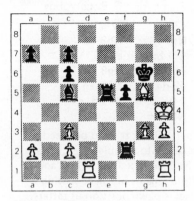

Black to move

White hits Black on the dark squares and sets up a standard mate.

1 Qd4xg7+   Kg8xg7

With his g-pawn gone Black has nothing with which he can defend the dark squares. White marches in.

2 Bg5-f6+   Kg7-g8
3 Rf4-h4

He is a queen ahead, but there is still nothing Black can do to stop mate on h8.

Score 5 points.

Black opens the lines for his bishop to hit the white king.

1 . . .   Rf2-f4+

White can now choose which diagonal he wants to be mated on!
(a)
2 g3xf4   Bc5-f2 mate
(b)
2 Bg5xf4   Bc5-e7+
3 Bf4-g5   Be7xg5 mate

Blocking the rook check is no better:
(c)
2 g3-g4   Bc5-f2 mate

Score 5 points.

Testgame 7

(*Ruy López*)
A. Flamberg   E. Bogolyubov

1	e2-e4	e7-e5
2	Ng1-f3	Nb8-c6
3	Bf1-b5	a7-a6
4	Bb5-a4	Ng8-f6
5	d2-d4	Nf6xe4
6	0-0	b7-b5
7	Nf3xe5	

Now if Black tries to be greedy
he gets into trouble: 7 . . .b5xa4
8 Ne5xc6 d7xc6 9 Rf1-e1 and
White regains his piece leaving
Black's pawn position in tatters.

7	...	Nc6xe5
8	d4xe5	

Q *What does Black do now?*

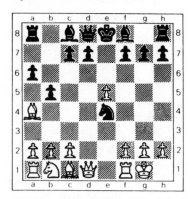

8	...	d7-d5

Score 3 points.
Black fights for the centre and
supports his knight.

Score 1 point for 8 . . . Bc8-b7,
but nothing for 8 . . .b5xa4 9
Qd1-d5 when White has a good
game.

9	e5xd6 e.p.	Bf8xd6
10	Ba4-b3	

Q *.Black is building up a K-side*
attack. How should he continue?

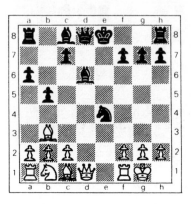

10	...	Bc8-b7

Score 3 points.
White has a solid pawn shield in
front of his king, but his pieces are
in no position to help defend.
Black's knight has a good central
square and his dark-squared bishop
is already sniping at h2.

    Black could be tempted to sail
straight in with his attack, but he
must complete his development
first. 10 . . .Bd6xh2+ isn't any good,
and 10 . . .Qd8-h4 11 g2-g3 Qh4-h3
is answered by 12 Qd1-d5. By
playing his bishop to b7 Black
defends d5 and his knight, and he
brings his bishops together to
scythe across the board at the
enemy king position.

11	a2-a4	0-0
12	a4xb5	

Q *What does Black play now?*

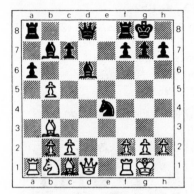

12 ...   Qd8-h4

Score 3 points.
His pieces are ready; so Black
opens fire. The first salvo threatens
mate at h2.

Score 1 point for 12 . . .a6xb5
which gets back the pawn — Black
is after more!

13 h2-h3

Black's queen and bishop have
forced White to weaken the castle
wall. The alternative for White, 13
g2-g3, would have left all the sentry
pawns on dark squares. Black's
queen and queen's bishop would
then have had a field day invading
the light ones!

13 ...   Ne4xf2!

A gaping hole appears in the castle
wall at g3 . . . now Black's queen
and king's bishop will have a
field day on the dark squares!

14 Rf1xf2

Q *How does Black continue the attack?*

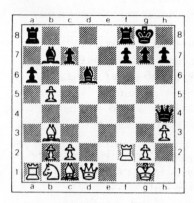

14 ...   Bd6-c5

Score 3 points.
Black sets up a deadly pin as the
second salvo threatens f2.

15 Qd1-f1   Ra8-e8

Black grabs an open file, threatening 16 . . .Bc5xf2+ and 17
. . .Re8-e1+. The pin is beginning
to look rather nasty!

16 Bc1-d2   Re8-e5
17 Ra1-a4

Q *How does Black save his queen?*

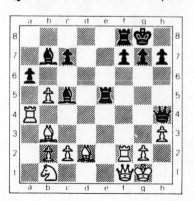

17 ...   **Qh4-e7**

Score 3 points.

Black prepares to blast his way
down the open file, and he lines
his third salvo up on e1.

Score 1 point for 17 ...Qh4xf2+.
No score for 17 ... Qh4-g3. Keeping the pressure on the dark squares
would be a good idea, but the queen
gets embarrassed by 18 Ra4-g4.

Take 2 points off your score if you
suggested 17 ...Qh4-f6 when
White plays 18 Bd2-c3 and gets his
own pin!

18 b5xa6   **Bb7xa6!**

The battle will be decided on the
weak dark squares around the white
king. Black sacrifices his other
bishop to lure the white queen
away.

19 Qf1xa6

Q *How does Black continue the
attack?*

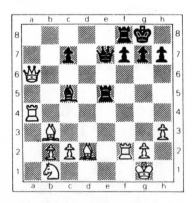

19 ...   **Re5-e1+!**

Score 5 points.

Black invades, and the white rook,
paralysed on f2, is first for the chop!

20 Kg1-h2

If 20 Bd2xe1 Qe7xe1+ 21 Qa6-f1
Bc5xf2+, White's queen and king
get chopped as well!

20 ...   **Bc5xf2**

21 Nb1-c3

Q *What should Black do now?*

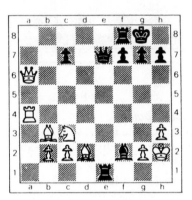

21 ...   **Qe7-e5+**

Score 3 points.

Black keeps up the barrage on the
dark-squared diagonals. The white
sentry pawns idly guard the light
squares and leave their king to take
the battering alone.

22 Ra4-f4

There was nothing else White could
try; 22 g2-g3 Qe5xg3 was mate,
and 22 Bd2-f4 Re1-h1+ 23 Kh2xh1
Qe5-e1+ with mate to follow on g1.

22 ...   **g7-g5**

23 Qa6-b5

Q *How does Black finish off the attack?*

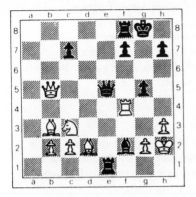

23 ...   g5xf4

Score 5 points.

The pawn has trundled up to attack the hole on g3. Black now threatens to mate by 24 . . .Bf2-g3.

24   Bd2xe1

Q *Now what should Black do?*

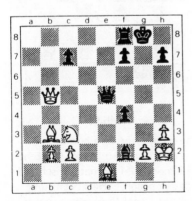

24 ...   Bf2-g3+

Score 4 points.

The final salvo! Black occupies the hole and it's all over.

Take 4 points off your score if you were going to play 24 . . . Qe5xe1. White then plays 25 Qb5-g5+ and gets a draw, since Black can't stop him checking on f6 and g5. Don't forget that whilst Black may be winning White is still playing.

25   Be1xg3   f4xg3+
26   Kh2-g1

Q *Find Black's next move.*

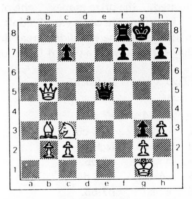

26 ...   Qe5-e3+

Score 3 points.
Nothing for 26 . . .Qe5-e1+ when White can block on f1 with his queen.

27   Kg1-h1   Qe3-e1+
28   Qb5-f1   Qe1xf1 mate

The winning method was simple. Black forced White to weaken his pawn shield. He then invaded the weak dark-squared diagonals and the white king had nowhere to hide.

'Gee, terrific!'

1943. . .born Chicago, U.S.A. . . .name, Robert James Fischer.
1956. . .Junior Champion of U.S.A. . . .youngest ever winner.
1957. . .Champion of the U.S.A. . . . youngest ever winner.
1958. . .International Grandmaster. . .youngest ever title holder.
1959. . .candidate for World Championship. . .youngest ever challenger.
1970. . .unofficial World Lightning Champion.
1971. . .World Championship candidates' winner.
1972. . .World Champion!

Champion of the World, and possibly the strongest ever chess-player, yet Bobby was just as famous for his behaviour off the board. Bobby found a few things to complain about in his time. . .the Russians who cheated. . .the prize money. . .the playing conditions. . .

To be fair the chess world didn't always treat Bobby kindly. One day in 1963 someone else didn't treat Bobby too kindly either. . .a guy called Burger armed with a pair of torpedoes.

(*Two Knights Defence*)

	Fischer	Burger
1	e2-e4	e7-e5
2	Ng1-f3	Nb8-c6
3	Bf1-c4	Ng8-f6
4	Nf3-g5	d7-d5
5	e4xd5	Nc6-d4
6	c2-c3	b7-b5
7	Bc4-f1	Nf6xd5
8	c3xd4	Qd8xg5
9	Bf1xb5+	Ke8-d8
10	Qd1-f3	Bc8-b7

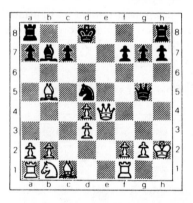

First torpedo in position.

11	0-0	e5-e4
12	Qf3xe4	Bf8-d6

Second tube loaded!

13	d2-d3	Bd6xh2+

Fischer is holed below the waterline.

14 Kg1xh2

Or 14 Kg1-h1 Bh2-f4 etc.

14 . . . Nd5-f4

The second torpedo homes in on e4 and g2. If now 15 Qe4xb7 Qg5-h5+ 16 Kh2-g1 Nf4-e2 mate. Fischer decides to resign. . .He's been sunk without trace! In fourteen moves.

Reports say Fischer's comment was "Gee, terrific!"
"*?-*!?*" would seem more likely!

Bishop blunders

Zurich 1953. The Candidates' Tournament for the World Championship.
In the White corner Laszlo Szabo, Hungarian grandmaster. In the Black
corner Samuel Reshevsky, grandmaster, champion of the U.S.A., and
leading Western challenger in a Russian-dominated event. The Russians
were happy. . .

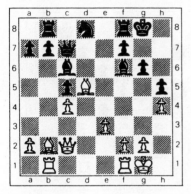

White to move

Szabo had just checked with his
knight on f6, and Reshevsky had
amazingly captured with the
bishop.
Everyone could see that Reshevsky's
f-pawn was pinned. Everyone . . .
except Szabo.
Szabo played:

1 Bb2xf6

He completely missed 1 Qc2xg6+
when Reshevsky could have cheer-
fully resigned. As it was he escaped
with a draw.

. . .the Russians were unhappy. How could Szabo have made such a
blunder? 'The worst blunder of the last decade' wrote Euwe. The
rumours came thick and fast from the Russian camp. . .Szabo had been
bribed! When asked to explain the mistake Szabo himself said it was easy,
'You just don't look for mates in two against Reshevsky.' Well, you should,
against anyone. Ten years later one of the Russians should have remembered Szabo.

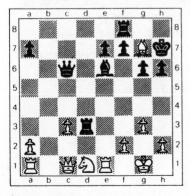

Black to move

Yuri Averbakh's move was obvious.
He should just have played 1 . . .
Kh7xg7 and he would have been
left with far the better position.
Averbakh was strong on the light
squares and he tried to be clever. . .

1 . . .   Be6-h3

. . .he got belted on the dark squares.

2 Qc1xh6+   Kh7-g8
3 Qh6-h8 mate

Even grandmasters make mistakes!

TEST EIGHT

Four problems to solve

Q *White can get a winning advantage with the help of a skewer. How?*

Q *White threatens 1 Qb5-e8 mate and 1 Nc5xe4. But it is Black who checkmates White! How?*

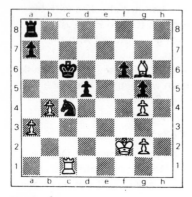

White to move

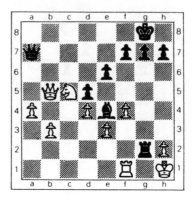

Black to move

Black's problems lie in his king and rook on the long diagonal. White wants his bishop on that diagonal, but first he must get rid of the black d-pawn.

1 Rc1xc4+   d5xc4
2 Bg6-e4+

The skewer! Black must move his king and leave his rook to be taken.

2 ...   Kc6-d6
3 Be4xa8

Score 2 points.

Black removes the troublesome knight and guards his first rank all in one go.

1 ...   Qa7xc5

The knight is gone and the black queen is ready to race back to f8.

2 d4xc5   Rg2-g3+
3 Rf1-f3   Be4xf3 mate

The white king has been tied up in his own corner.

Score 3 points.

Q *Black's queen stands on the long diagonal. Her reign is about to end! How does White win a piece?*

Q *Black has two splendid bishops. They both play a fine part in ending White's hopes. How?*

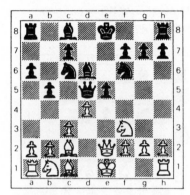

White to move

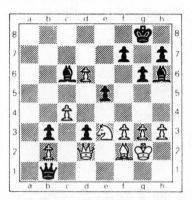

Black to move

Black's queen is short of space, and when she has gone he loses control of the long diagonal.

1 Bc2-b3

The queen is attacked and there is only one place to run. . .

1 . . .   Qd5-e4
2 Qe2xe4   Nf6xe4

Now White invades the diagonal.

3 Bb3-d5

The black knights are forked and one of them must fall.

Score 4 points.

White's queen and bishop stand on dark squares; so Black hits him hard on his weaker light squares.

1 . . .   Bc6xf3+
2 Kg2xf3

Or 2 Kg2-h2 Qb1-h1 mate.

2 . . .   Qb1-h1+

Now the other bishop plays its part; White can't block the check because his knight is pinned.

3 Kf3-g4   Qh1-e4 mate

Black's triumph on the light squares is complete.

Score 6 points.

Testgame 8

(*Caro-Kann Defence*)
R. Spielmann B. Honlinger

1	e2-e4	c7-c6
2	d2-d4	d7-d5
3	Nb1-c3	d5xe4
4	Nc3xe4	Ng8-f6
5	Ne4-g3	e7-e6
6	Ng1-f3	c6-c5
7	Bf1-d3	

Q *Can Black win a pawn now by 7 . . .c5xd4?*

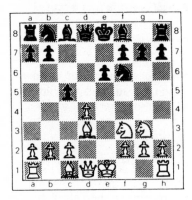

No.

Score 3 points.
After 7 . . .c5xd4 8 Nf3xd4
Qd8xd4 the white bishop hops out of the way and checks, 9 Bd3-b5+, and the black queen pays for her greed. Now, back to the game.

7	. . .	Nb8-c6
8	d4xc5	Bf8xc5
9	a2-a3	

White doesn't want his good light-squared bishop annoyed by 9 . . .Nc6-b4.

9	. . .	0-0
10	0-0	b7-b6
11	b2-b4	Bc5-e7

Q *How should White continue his development?*

12 Bc1-b2

Score 3 points.
The bishop finds a good home on the long diagonal, carving through the centre, and working with his partner to bombard the black king's stronghold.

Score 2 points for 12 Rf1-e1.
No score for 12 Bc1-f4 when the bishop will be driven off by a black knight on d5.

12	. . .	Qd8-c7
13	b4-b5	Nc6-a5

The black knight is kicked out to a horrible square. . .

14 Nf3-e5

. . .and White seizes an outpost in the centre.

14	. . .	Bc8-b7

Q *What does White do now?*

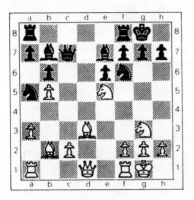

15 Ne5-g4

Score 4 points.
White is laying siege to the stronghold. He threatens to capture
twice on f6, doubling Black's
pawns on the f-file, and then invade through the shattered walls
with his queen and minor pieces.

Score 2 points for 15 Ng3-h5 or
15 Rf1-e1.

15 ...   Qc7-d8
16 Ng4-e3   Nf6-d5

Q *Now what should White do?*

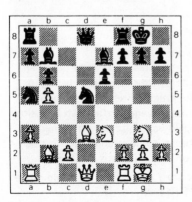

17 Qd1-h5

Score 4 points.
The bishops blaze away from a
distance and the queen homes in
on h7 with a mate threat.

Score 2 points for 17 Qd1-g4 or
17 Ng3-h5.

17 ...   g7-g6

The first cracks show in the black
position. He stops mate, he blunts
the power of White's light-squared
bishop, he attacks the white queen,
but . . .

Q *What is White's next move?*

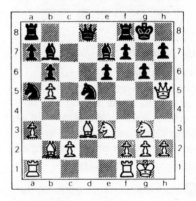

18 Ne3-g4!

Score 5 points.
Black's problem is that he has
given himself holes on f6 and h6,
and he has given White the full
length of the long diagonal for his
dark-squared bishop. White wastes
no time taking advantage; he
threatens 19 Ng4-h6 mate.

Score 1 point for 18 Qh5-h6.
Lose 2 points if you were going
to play 18 Qh5-e5; you lose a
bishop after 18 . . .Be7-f6.

18 ... Be7-f6

Q *How should White continue?*

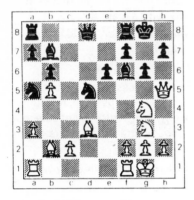

19 Ng4xf6+

Score 4 points.
Black's problems are on the dark squares, so White will hit him on the dark squares. White gets rid of Black's best defender and strengthens the power of his own bishop.

19 ... Nd5xf6

Q *Now the white queen really is threatened. Where should she go?*

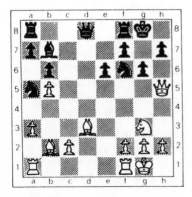

20 Qh5-h6

Score 2 points.

White keeps up the pressure on the dark squares. The black knight is now horribly pinned against the mate threat on g7.
No score for 20 Qh5-g5 or 20 Qh5-e5. Black's only real hope of a counter-attack lies on the long light-squared diagonal, and after 20 ...Qd8-d5 he threatens mate on g2 and forces White to exchange queens.

20 ... Ra8-c8

Q *What is White's next move?*

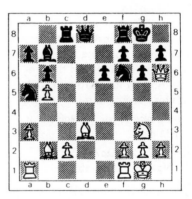

21 Ra1-d1

Score 3 points.
The two bishops sweep the board side by side, the queen is dug in, the knight is ready to spring into action. Siege warfare can be a slow business. White has no immediate threat; so he strengthens his position and threatens 22 Bd3xg6.

Score 1 point for the simple move 21 Rf1-e1.

21 ...   Qd8-e7
22 Rf1-e1

Another piece comes into play
and the black e-pawn is pinned.

22 ...   Nf6-e8

Black tries desperately to prop up
his weakened wall — defending
the dark squares, g7 and f6, is
better than sitting on them!

23 Ng3-f5

If Black takes this, 23 . . .g6xf5,
then 24 Bd3xf5 and the bishops
are murderous.

23 ...   Qe7-c5
24 Re1-e5   Bb7-d5
25 Nf5-e7+!

The start of a spectacular invasion
on the dark squares.

25 ...   Qc5xe7

Q *What is White's killer blow?*

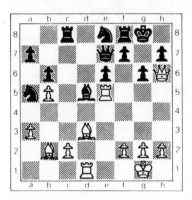

26 Qh6xh7+!!

Score 5 points.
White invades and brings his light-
squared bishop into the game
with a nasty pin.

26 ...   Kg8xh7

Q *How does White finish it off?*

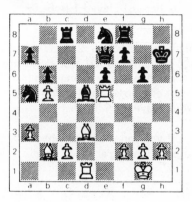

27 Re5-h5+

Score 2 points.

27 ...   Kh7-g8

His g-pawn pinned Black can only
run away. . .but there is nowhere
to go!

28 Rh5-h8 mate

Black has collapsed on the dark
squares, and the white rook has
cashed in on the power of his
bishops.

Once again two bishops, side by
side, proved a devastating weapon.
The light-squared bishop helped to
weaken Black's king position, the
dark-squared bishop led the invasion on the weakened squares.
The loss of his own king's bishop
left Black unable to defend himself. White patiently built up his
forces before lifting his own siege
and smashing through the enemy
wall.

A bishop is worth...

White has just played **1 Rc6-c8+**.

Why?

After 1 . . . Kb8xc8 2 b6-b7+
Kc8-b8 3 b7xa8=Q+ Kb8xa8 White
has no chance of winning, and he
might even lose! So, *why has
White played 1 Rc6-c8+?*

See if you can work out why,
without looking at the answer
below.

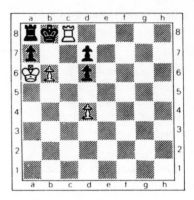

Black to move

The first two moves are forced:

1 . . .	Kb8xc8
2 b6-b7+	Kc8-b8
3 d4-d5!	

The point! Black can only move
his king.

3 . . .   **Kb8-c7**

And now White can capture the
rook, promote his pawn to a
queen, and win easily.
Can't he?
No! He can't.

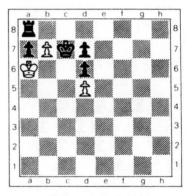

Position after 3 . . .Kb8-c7

If White captures and promotes his pawn to a queen, Black is stalemated.
If White captures and promotes to a rook it is still stalemate.
If White captures and promotes to a knight, Black simply plays 4 . . . Kc7-b8
and takes the knight next move.
White must promote to a bishop!

4 b7xa8=B

Now if 4 . . .Kc7-b8 5 Ba8-b7 Kb8-c7 6 Ka6xa7 and White wins easily.

... more than it seems

The last position should give you
a clue to this.

The question is, how does White
avoid losing?

(Don't forget: White is going up
the board!)

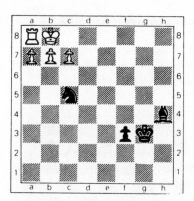

White to move

To begin with White can't queen
his c-pawn: 1 c7-c8=Q Nc5-a6
mate. So White must move his
king.

1 Kb8-c8   f3-f2

Now White can't move his king:
2 Kc8-b8 f2-f1=Q and mate next
move.

He can't move his rook:
2 Ra8-b8 f2-f1=Q and Black
mates on f8.

He can't queen his pawn:
2 b7-b8=Q f2-f1=Q and Black
threatens mate on f8, f5, h3,
and a6.

Position after 1 . . .f3-f2

What can White do? Every move seems to lose.
The clue from the last position is *the bishop*.

2 b7-b8=B

Now the nice new bishop can't go anywhere, and White has carefully
stalemated himself. If Black queens his pawn, or moves his king, or
moves his bishop, the game is drawn. If he moves his knight the white
king can escape on d7, White will then queen his c-pawn and may even win!
There is nothing Black can do! He must allow the stalemate.

TEST NINE

Four problems to solve

Q *The white king is trapped on the long diagonal. How does Black finish him off?*

Q *White's bishop can discover check in several ways. Which way leads to checkmate?*

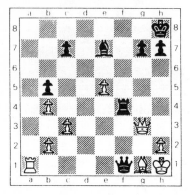

Black to move

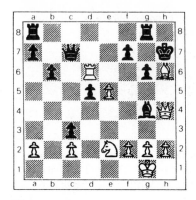

White to move

The black queen forces her way on to the diagonal.

1 . . .   Qf1xa1

Unless White wishes to battle on a rook down, he must recapture.

2 Qg3xf4   Qa1-a8+

The diagonal is seized and the king neatly trapped.

3 Qf4-f3   Qa8xf3 mate

Score 2 points.

The black king must be trapped in his corner.

1 Bh6-f8+   Bg4-h5

The black bishop seems to have come to the rescue. But. . .

2 Qh4xh5+

. . .he gets smashed aside.

2 . . .   g6xh5

3 Rd6-h6 mate

Score 3 points.

Q *Black's bishop seems to defend the weak dark squares around his king. How does White invade?*

Q *Black has a fierce K-side attack. But it is White, thanks to his two bishops, who checkmates. How?*

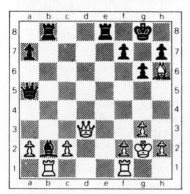

White to move

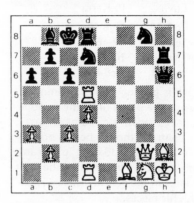

White to move

White destroys the defender.

1 Rb1xb2   Rb8xb2
2 Qd3-d4

White grabs the long diagonal and threatens the rook on b2 and mate on g7.

2 . . .   Qa5-e5

Black fights for the diagonal; the only way he can defend against both threats.

3 Rf1-e1

The end!
If Black moves his queen off the diagonal he is mated on g7 (3 . . . Qe5xe1 4 Qd4-g7 mate). If Black stays on the diagonal he is mated on the back rank (3 . . .Qe5xd4 4 Re1xe8 mate).

Score 4 points.

The two bishops rake the Q-side and set up a standard mate. White only has to get rid of the pawn on b7.

1 Rd5-h5

The rook is sacrificed to make way for the queen.

1 . . .   Qh6xh5
2 Qg2xc6+

Another brilliant sacrifice to break up the black pawns.

2 . . .   b7xc6
3 Bf1xa6 mate

Score 6 points.

Testgame 9

(*Queen's Indian Defence*)

M. Euwe	P. Keres
1 d2-d4	Ng8-f6
2 c2-c4	e7-e6
3 Ng1-f3	b7-b6
4 g2-g3	Bc8-b7

Black is playing a quiet opening, leaving the battle until the middle-game. He doesn't put a pawn in the centre, although he can do so by either . . .d7-d5 or . . .c7-c5 any time he likes. He is hitting the light squares in the centre, especially e4, with his pieces.

5 Bf1-g2	Bf8-e7
6 0-0	0-0
7 Nb1-c3	Nf6-e4
8 Qd1-c2	Ne4xc3
9 Qc2xc3	d7-d6
10 Qc3-c2	

White plans to seize more of the centre by 11 e2-e4.

Q *How should Black hold up White's plan?*

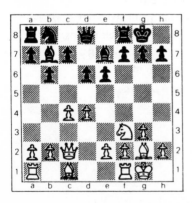

10 . . .   f7-f5

Score 4 points.

Black hits e4 again. The alternative way, 10 . . . d6-d5, blocks the long diagonal and leaves the bishop shut in after the pawns are exchanged.

Score 1 point for the developing move 10 . . .Nb8-c6.

11 Nf3-e1	Qd8-c8
12 e2-e4	Nb8-d7
13 d4-d5	f5xe4
14 Qc2xe4	

Q *Black comes under fire on e6. What should he do?*

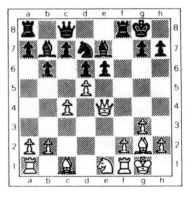

14 . . .   Nd7-c5

Score 4 points.

Black doubly defends his e-pawn and attacks the white queen.

Score 0 points for 14 . . .e6-e5. This saves your pawn but costs your bishops dearly. The dark-squared bishop is trapped behind his own pawns on d6 and e5; his partner is blunted by the white pawn blockade on d5. Here, as always, the power of the bishops depends upon the position of the pawns.

Lose 2 points if you would have played 14 . . .e6xd5, leaving your bishop on e7 *en prise.*

15 Qe4-e2

Q *Now what should Black do?*

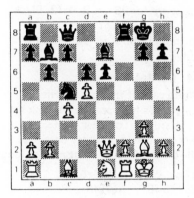

15 . . .   Be7-f6

Score 4 points.
The bishop seizes a good diagonal from which he can attack the centre. He pins the white b-pawn and saves his knight from the embarrassment of 16 b2-b4. He invites his rook to come to e8.

Score 1 point for 15 . . .a7-a5.

16 Bg2-h3

Black's weaknesses are clear: e6 and the light-squared diagonals leading into the heart of his position.

16 . . .   Rf8-e8

Black's strength is equally clear: good development, with particularly well-placed minor pieces. He threatens simply 17 . . .e6xd5.

17 Bc1-e3   Qc8-d8

Breaking the pin.

18 Be3xc5   e6xd5

The only way to save his e-pawn. If now 19 Bc5-e3, Black wins back his piece by 19 . . .d5-d4.

19 Bh3-e6+   Kg8-h8
20 Ra1-d1   d6xc5
21 Ne1-g2

Q *What is Black's next move?*

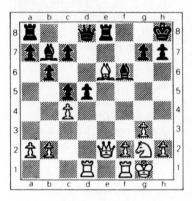

21 . . .   d5-d4

Score 2 points.
With an extra pawn and two good bishops Black takes his chance to get a passed pawn. He opens up the long diagonal for his light-squared bishop — but he shuts in his other bishop.

Score 4 points for 21 . . .Bf6-d4. With this move Black would block the d-file. He could then exchange his d-pawn for the white c-pawn, and his two bishops, beautifully placed on an open board, would have a field day!

Score 2 points for 21 . . .Qd8-d6.

22 f2-f4   d4-d3!

Black quickly makes up for his mistake and sacrifices a pawn to bring his king's bishop back to life.

23 Rd1xd3   Qd8xd3!!

All part of the plan, but Black doesn't seem to be getting enough for his queen.

24 Qe2xd3   Bf6-d4+
25 Rf1-f2

If White puts his king in the corner, 25 Kg1-h1, then Black plays 25 ...Re8xe6, 26 ...Ra8-e8, and 27 ...Re6-e2, and the corner becomes a death trap.

25 ...   Re8xe6

The smoke has cleared, and Black has a rook and a bishop for his queen. Not enough. But! Look at the bishops. They stand astride the centre, carving a motorway into White's position, and more than make up for the material loss.

26 Kg1-f1

Q *How does Black keep up the attack?*

26 ...   Ra8-e8

Score 4 points.
All Black's pieces have sprung into action. He has total control of the open file, although White is desperately guarding the invasion points. Black also has his two bishops!

No score for 26 ... Bd4xf2. Black wouldn't dream of giving up one of those bishops for White's miserable rook!

27 f4-f5

White cannot find a plan. His knight has to guard e1, his rook has to guard e2. Together the two pieces make up a flimsy barrier to the black bishops. . .but not for long.

27 ...   Re6-e5
28 f5-f6   g7xf6
29 Rf2-d2

If White had recaptured, his rook really would have fallen to the bishop: 29 Rf2xf6 Bb7xg2+ 30 Kf1xg2 Re5-e2+, and 31 ... Bd4xf6.

Q *Now what should Black do?*

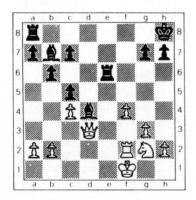

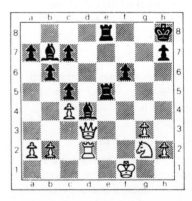

29 . . .   Bb7-c8!!

Score 6 points.

The long diagonal, along which the light-squared bishop has breathed fire for so long, has served its use. The white king has fled towards the centre. The black bishop looks for new lines of attack and threatens to go to h3 where it will pin down the white knight.

30 Ng2-f4

The threat of the pin forces the knight out of g2 and gives the black rooks invasion squares on the open e-file.

30 . . .   Re6-e3

Checking on e1 was also good.

31 Qd3-b1   Re3-f3+
32 Kf1-g2

Q *Black strikes brilliantly. How?*

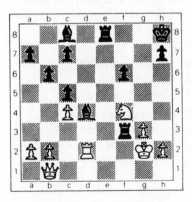

32 . . .   Rf3xf4!

Score 5 points.

White's only well-placed piece is destroyed. Black now has only the

two bishops for his queen — but those two bishops own all the squares!

33 g3xf4   Re8-g8+
34 Kg2-f3

Q *How does Black finish it off?*

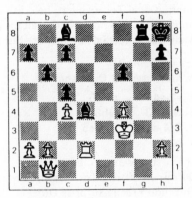

34 . . .   Bc8-g4+

Score 4 points.

The bishops bombard the central squares and the white royal family get caught in the cross-fire. Euwe decided he'd been battered enough at this point and resigned. A pity! Just when the light-squared bishop was enjoying himself. If Euwe had tried 35 Kf3-g3 Bg4-f5+ and the bishop clobbers the white queen. And if Euwe had tried 35 Kf3-e4 Rg8-e8+ the bishop would have mated him.

The game was really decided by the pawn battle in the centre. Keres won the battle and kept his pawns out of the way of his bishops. The sudden devastating end showed just how terrible the power of two bishops can be on an open board.

Dufresne's birthday party

Berlin, 1852. It was definitely not Dufresne's birthday. It wasn't Christmas either. So, why was Dufresne getting so many presents? His opponent seemed to be showering him with pieces. Very strange. Even more strange when Dufresne considered who he was playing. Adolf Anderssen was supposed to be the strongest player in the world; he had won the first ever International Tournament, held in London the year before. So, what was Anderssen up to now? Giving all his pieces away. . .except for his bishops. What was so special about those bishops?

(*Evans Gambit*)
A. Anderssen   J. Dufresne

1	e2-e4	e7-e5
2	Ng1-f3	Nb8-c6
3	Bf1-c4	Bf8-c5
4	b2-b4	

The first present comes through Dufresne's letter box. A pawn! This didn't really surprise Dufresne. The English naval captain W.D. Evans had invented this gambit opening in 1824, and it had been popular with attacking players ever since.

4	. . .	Bc5xb4
5	c2-c3	Bb4-a5
6	d2-d4	e5xd4
7	0-0	

Before Dufresne had time to say thank you properly for the first present, a second pawn arrives, gift-wrapped.

7	. . .	d4-d3

This one Dufresne wasn't so sure about. If he had taken the pawn a white knight would have ended up on c3 hammering at the centre. Anyway, Dufresne hadn't realized yet that it was going to be his birthday!

8	Qd1-b3	Qd8-f6
9	e4-e5	

A third pawn is presented.

9	. . .	Qf6-g6

Dufresne didn't like that one either. After 9 . . .Nc6xe5 10 Rf1-e1 d7-d6 11 Qb3-b5+ he loses his bishop.

10	Rf1-e1	Ng8-e7
11	Bc1-a3	b7-b5

With two pawns in the bag Dufresne can afford to give one of them back to slow his opponent down and finish off his own development.

12	Qb3xb5	Ra8-b8
13	Qb5-a4	Ba5-b6
14	Nb1-d2	Bc8-b7

All seems to be going quite well for Dufresne; his position looks solid and he's got his pieces into play. The pawn on e5 is a bit of a nuisance and those two white bishops look menacing, but all Anderssen has done so far is to wave his pawns about like confetti.

15	Nd2-e4	Qg6-f5
16	Bc4xd3	

Dufresne is looking bored.

Anderssen decides to liven things up. He threatens 17 Ne4-f6+ winning the black queen.

16 ...   Qf5-h5
17 Ne4-f6+

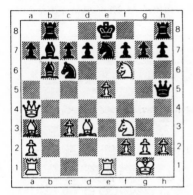

The party is under way!

17 ...   g7xf6

Dufresne unwraps this present with great glee. He gets a knight and the open g-file.

18 e5xf6   Rh8-g8
19 Ra1-d1

The other white knight is offered!

19 ...   Qh5xf3

Dufresne grabs everything that's going. He has two extra knights, the open g-file, and he threatens mate on g2.

20 Re1xe7+

Yet another present! Dufresne can hardly believe his luck. Perhaps it is his birthday after all.

20 ...   Nc6xe7
21 Qa4xd7+

A parcel bomb! Dufresne finds he's got one present he didn't want.

21 ...   Ke8xd7
22 Bd3-f5++ Kd7-e8

Or 22...Kd7-c6 23 Bf5-d7 mate. Dufresne has a queen, a rook, and a knight more. But the music has stopped...something seems to be going wrong with his party.

23 Bf5-d7+

The gatecrasher! A bishop arrives uninvited to spoil Dufresne's fun.

23 ...   Ke8-d8
24 Ba3xe7 mate

A second bishop turns his birthday party into a funeral!

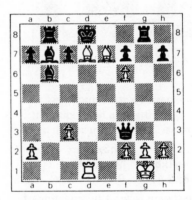

Two beautiful bishops!

Dufresne had found out the hard way just why Anderssen was considered the strongest player in the world. In an age of gambit openings and wild sacrificial attacks Anderssen was the master executioner. His opponents had to die properly. Death should be dealt out with dash and daring. Anderssen didn't just beat them...he smashed them!

TEST TEN

Four problems to solve

Q *Black can sacrifice to smash open the h-file and checkmate the white king. How?*

Q *Black is in check. He has three ways out: two will lose, one will win. How does Black win a piece?*

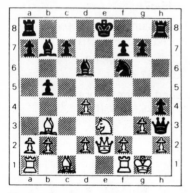

Black to move

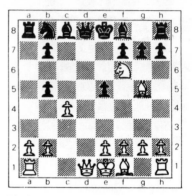

Black to move

Black has two attacking lines: the h-file and the long light-squared diagonal. The lines meet at h1.

1	...	Qh3xh2+
2	Kg1xh2	h4xg3++
3	Kh2-g1	Rh8-h1 mate

The rook arrives at the meeting of the lines!

Score 2 points.

The obvious 1 . . .g7xf6 is disastrous after 2 Qd1xd8+ Ke8xd8 3 Bg5xf6+. Moving the king also loses; 1 . . .Ke8-e7 2 Nf6-d5++. The way to win is:

1	...	Qd8xf6
2	Bg5xf6	Bf8-b4+

And now it's the white queen who is in trouble.

3	Qd1-d2	Bb4xd2+
4	Ke1xd2	g7xf6

The dust has settled and Black has an extra knight!

Score 3 points.

Q *The white queen is free on an open board. How does she help force a quick win?*

Q *White has two good bishops and several attacking lines. How does he finish Black off?*

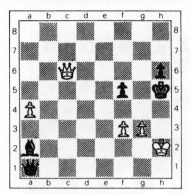

White to move

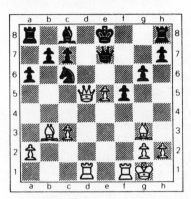

White to move

The white queen can weave an evil path on the diagonals.

1 Qc6-e8+   Kh5-g5
2 f3-f4+

Now Black can choose which to lose: his king or his queen!

(a)

2 ...   Kg5-g4
3 Qe8-e2 mate

(b)

2 ...   Kg5-f6
3 Qe8-h8+

Score 4 points.

The black queen is overloaded; she has to defend f7 and d8.

1 Bg3-h4

White grabs a good diagonal. If Black takes he is mated on f7.

1 ...   Qe7-g7
2 Qd5-d8+   Nc6xd8
3 Rd1xd8 mate

The black king is caught in the bishops' cross-fire.

Score 6 points.

Testgame 10

(*Caro–Kann Defence*)
Chalupetzky   Kallos

1	e2-e4	c7-c6
2	c2-c4	d7-d5
3	e4xd5	c6xd5
4	c4xd5	Qd8xd5
5	Nb1-c3	Qd5-d8
6	Bf1-c4	

Good development, hitting the
weak point at f7.

6	...	Ng8-f6
7	d2-d4	g7-g6

Q *How should White continue
developing?*

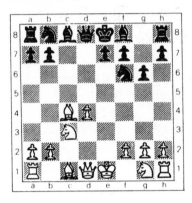

8 Qd1-b3!

Score 4 points.
White keeps up the pressure on f7,
and forces Black to move his e-pawn.

Score 2 points if you were going to
develop your knight on f3 or e2.

Score 1 point if you were going to
develop your dark-squared bishop
on e3, f4, or g5.

8	...	e7-e6

Forced. But now Black has all his
K-side pawns on light squares.

Q *What should White do now?*

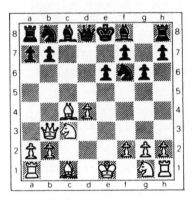

9 Bc1-g5

Score 3 points.
Black has weakened the dark
squares; so White hits them straight
away with a nasty pin.

Score 1 point for 9 Ng1-f3, or 9
Ng1-e2.

9	...	Bf8-g7

Q *White has a lead in development.
What should he do now?*

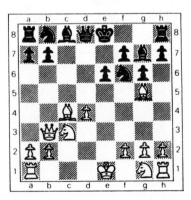

10 d4-d5

Score 4 points.

The black pawn on e6 is a road-block to White's power on the light-squared diagonal. It is dynamited. White, with the better development, will get the advantage when the position is opened up.

Score 2 points for 10 Ng1-f3 or 10 0-0-0.

10 ... e6xd5

Q *What does White play now?*

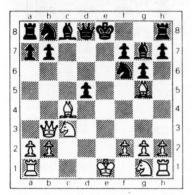

11 0-0-0

Score 4 points.

More development and another pin. Rather than recapture immediately White keeps up the pressure.

Score 2 points for 11 Nc3xd5. *Nothing* for 11 Bc4xd5; on the open board White doesn't want to risk having either of his splendid bishops exchanged.

11 ... 0-0
12 Nc3xd5 Nb8-d7
13 Ng1-f3

White plans 14 Nf3-e5 (Black can't capture, 14 ...Nd7xe5 15 Nd5xf6+

costs him his queen), and 15 Ne5-g4. The pin on f6 is beginning to bite; White's lead in development is growing.

13 ... Qd8-a5
14 Bg5-d2! Qa5-d8

Q *How should White keep up the pressure?*

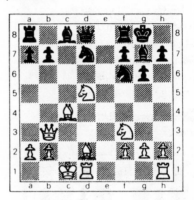

15 Bd2-b4

Score 4 points.

There is nothing more to be gained from the pin; so White switches the bishop and finds a new target. The two white bishops join forces. The light-squared one, aided by the queen, hits f7. The dark-squared one drives away the black rook.

Score 2 points for keeping up the attack on f7 by 15 Nf3-g5, and *1 point* for the sensible developing move 15 Rh1-e1.

15 ... Rf8-e8
16 Rh1-e1

The open e-file will be White's invasion route. He completes his development, exchanges Black's active rook, and grabs the file.

16	...	Re8xe1
17	Rd1xe1	Nf6xd5
18	Bc4xd5	Qd8-c7+
19	Qb3-c4!	Qc7xc4+
20	Bd5xc4	

White is left with his lead in development, his open file, and . . . his magnificent battery of bishops.

20	...	Nd7-f8
21	Re1-e8	

White invades the back rank and keeps the black bishop at home.

| 21 | ... | Bg7-h6+ |

Q *How does White get out of check?*

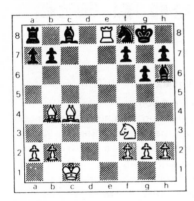

22 Kc1-d1

Score 2 points.

Lose 3 points if you were going to play 22 Kc1-b1 or 22 Kc1-c2. After 22 . . .Bc8-f5+ your rook on e8 looks a bit stupid! Black has bishops as well!

22	...	a7-a6
23	Kd1-e1	

White wants to play Nf3-g5, but he

daren't allow . . .Bc8-g4+.

23	...	a6-a5
24	Bb4-d6	b7-b6

Q *How does White continue his attack?*

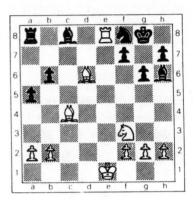

25 Nf3-e5

Score 3 points.

Score 3 points also for 25 Bc4-d5 which wins the exchange after 25 . . .Bc8-b7 26 Re8xa8.

25	...	Bc8-b7
26	Bb3xf7+	Kg8-h8

Q *What does White do now?*

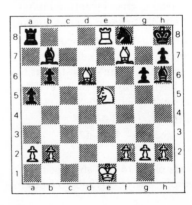

27 Re8-e7

Score 3 points.
The rook finds new targets on the seventh rank.
Score 1 point for 27 Re8xa8.
White might win the ending with his extra pawn, but why exchange an active rook for a useless one?

27 . . .   Bb7xg2
28 Bf7-c4

The white pieces are gathering like storm clouds over the black king. They must be sorted out into battle order. The two bishops work powerfully together, but the dark-squared one would be better on the long diagonal.

28 . . .   Bh6-g7
29 Ne5-f7+   Kh8-g8
30 Nf7-d8+   Kg8-h8

Q *What is White's next move?*

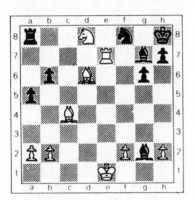

31 Re7xg7!

Score 5 points.
One flash of lightning: one clap of thunder, and it's all over. The black bishop which defended the dark

squares is struck down. The white bishops pour in like a torrent.

31 . . .   Kh8xg7
32 Bd6-e5+   Kg7-h6
33 Nd8-f7+   Kh6-h5
34 Bc4-e2+   Kh5-h4

Q *The white pieces control all the squares. How do they finish the job?*

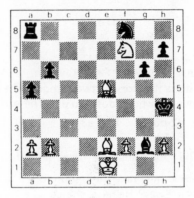

35 Be5-g3+

Score 3 points.
The white pieces weave a net around the black king . . . there is no escape.

35 . . .   Kh4-h3
36 Nf7-g5 mate

Two bishops operating together, a powerful strike force. The light-squared bishop and the queen forced Black to weaken his pawn position. The dark-squared bishop hammered in with the pin. Black struggled, he lost time, he fell behind in development. The bishops joined forces side by side; they hit f7 and f8. The rook was sacrificed to destroy Black's last foothold on the dark squares. Then the bishops took over!

Buried alive

You might think that Black has a
good chance of winning this position.
He hasn't.
All Black does have is a choice. He
can choose which king he wants
to bury alive!

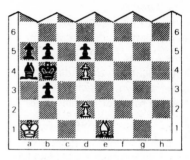

White to move

This is the story of two bishops. The good white one, full of life and
squares, who chooses to die. The bad black one — who's dead anyway!

1 d2-d3+   Kb4-a3
2 Be1-b4+

The good bishop sacrifices himself to save the game.

Black must take the bishop. But
which way? He has a choice. . . a
rotten choice!
(a) Black can play:

2 . . .   Ka3xb4
3 Ka1-b2

When he suddenly finds he has
stalemated himself.

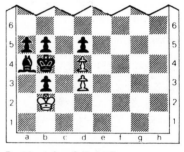

Position after 3 Ka1-b2

(b) or Black can play:

2 . . .   a5xb4
3 Ka1-b1

Then he must play:

3 . . .   b3-b2

And now he suddenly finds he
has managed to stalemate White!

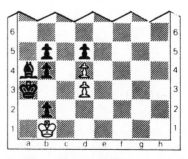

Position after 3 . . .b3-b2

The black king's beauty parade

It was time he got married. The black king was sure of that. The problem was *who* to marry? Four sweet little pawns were queueing up on the seventh rank to become his queen. Which one should he choose? He must be careful, as king he couldn't just take any old hag for his wife. What he needed was a closer inspection of the candidates. It really was a problem.

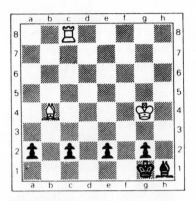

White to move

That was where the white pieces gave a hand. They invited the king on a guided tour. In fact they didn't so much invite him as drive him!

1 Bb4-c5+

The black king has been eyeing up Miss g-pawn for long enough, it's time he moved on.

1 ...   Kg1-f1
2 Rc8-f8+   Kf1-e1

Ah! Miss e-pawn, very nice. . . bit skinny though.

3 Bc5-b4+   Ke1-d1
4 Rf8-d8+   Kd1-c1

Hullo! Miss c-pawn eh? Yes. . .

5 Bb4-a3+   Kc1-b1

Wait a minute, wait a minute! Give me time to think. . .you can't rush these things.

6 Rd8-b8+   Kb1-a1

Cor! You're Miss a-pawn are you? You look just. . .

7 Ba3-b2+   Ka1-b1

Hey where are we going now? I hadn't finished with Miss a-pawn.

8 Bb2-e5+   Kb1-c1

Oh, back for a second look. Well, that can't be a bad idea.

9   Be5-f4+   Kc1-d1
10 Rb8-d8+   Kd1-e1
11 Bf4-g3+   Ke1-f1
12 Rd8-f8+   Kf1-g1

Back where we started then. Right, decision time. Now. . .

13 Kg4-h3

. . .I think. . .Yes, Miss a-pawn, sweet shy little thing. She'll do well. . .got a smashing fi. . . .

13 ...   a2-a1=Q

Excited by the Parade, the black king has missed the point. It is not he, it is the white bishop who is judge, jury. . .

14 Bg3-h2 mate

. . .and executioner!

The power of the pin

Try to work out how White can win from this position. Don't be surprised if you get dizzy on the diagonals! Black has to walk into two horrible pins.

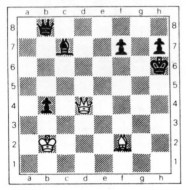

White to move

1	Qd4-f6+	Kh6-h5
2	Qf6-f5+	Kh5-h6
3	Bf2-e3+	Kh6-g7
4	Qf5-g5+	Kg7-f8

If 4 . . . Kg7-h8, 5 Be3-d4+ wins.

5 Be3-c5+ Bc7-d6

If 5 . . . Kf8-e8, 6 Qg5-e7 is mate.

6 Qg5-e5

Pin one. The black bishop daren't move . . . but he's dead where he is!

6	. . .	Qb8-d8
7	Bc5xd6+	Kf8-g8
8	Qe5-g3+	Kg8-h8
9	Bd6-e5+	f7-f6

And now, same again!

10 Qg3-g5

Pin two. Black is crucified!

A bishop out of the blue

Black's a-pawn is on the march, but. . .

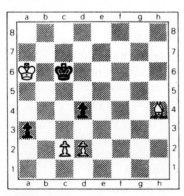

White to move

1 Bh4-f6 Kc6-d5

Not 1 . . . Kc6-c5 2 Bf6-e7+ winning the black a-pawn.

2	d2-d3	a3-a2
3	c2-c4+	Kd5-c5

As long as Black's d-pawn blocks the long diagonal his a-pawn can march safely forward.

4 Ka6-b7 a2-a1=Q

Black's a-pawn has made it to the coronation. The new queen is enthroned on a1. The old king is belted by a thunderbolt on c5! A bishop out of the blue!

5 Bf6-e7 mate!

Neat!

Raiding knights

Knights go into attack as raiders. Queens, rooks, and bishops can sit safely at home and bombard the enemy from afar. Knights cannot. Knights are short-range pieces; they cannot reach out across the board. They must raid the enemy's position, get to grips with him face to face, and slug it out at close quarters.

A knight exerts all his power on the squares close by him. For this reason a knight is generally better placed in the centre, where he can switch from side to side, spring to the attack or turn to the defence. A knight who has invaded the centre of the enemy position can be a tremendous attacking weapon.

Here the white knight has raided deep into enemy territory. He swivels to fire in all directions. He hits the pawns on f7 and b7, and he stops Black from putting a rook on e8 or c8. He can go to b5 and threaten the black queen, or he can retreat to e4 and switch to a K-side attack.

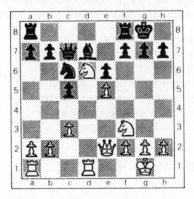

The knight has seized a superb base from which to operate.

As a raider the knight will come under enemy fire. He cannot hope to invade the enemy position without being attacked. The knight needs an operations base from which he cannot easily be kicked out. In the position above he has that base. He is firmly supported by his own pawn on e5, and the black pawns can't get at him.

Getting a good base from which to operate is generally easier in closed positions where there are plenty of pawns on the board. In positions where there are open lines a knight cannot expect to dig himself in. The pawns will not be there to defend him; he will have to rely upon pieces for support. He will need to flit around and fight the hit-and-run battle of a true raider.

The two main tactical strengths of the knight are the fork and the discovered attack.

The fork
In a fork the knight attacks two enemy pieces at the same time. The enemy, unable to have two moves running, is able to save only one of his pieces.

White's knight forks Black's king and rook

You must always be on the look-out for squares from which your knight might be able to make a double attack. Sometimes you will find an easy, simple fork. More often you will have to do a little work first.

Here the important square is d6. From d6 the white knight will fork e4 and f7. If he goes to d6 straight away the knight will attack the black queen and thin air! White must set up the fork by driving out the black king:

1 Rc3-c8+   Kg8-f7

Now White is ready. . .

2 Nb5-d6+

. . .and Black loses his queen.

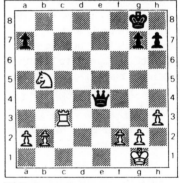

White to move

Here f5 looks a good home for the knight. The trouble is that f5 is heavily defended. White destroys the defenders and sets up the fork:

1 Qe2xh5   g6xh5

Now the gate is open. . .

2 Ne3-f5+

. . .and White comes out a rook ahead.

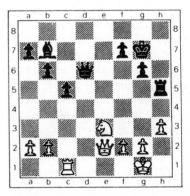

White to move

The discovered attack

A knight sometimes finds himself blocking the line of attack of another piece. When he moves out of the way the knight opens the line and discovers the attack.

Here the white knight blocks his queen's line of attack. When the knight moves Black will be in check. White plays:

1 Ne5-c6+

The attack is discovered. The e-file is open and Black is in check. At the same time the black queen is threatened. Black, too busy dealing with the check, cannot save his queen.

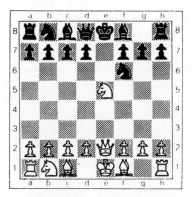

White to move

Discovering an attack gives a knight the chance to do some real raiding. He can take up a death-defying position, yet be perfectly safe. In the position above the knight could also go to g6. Again he would be attacked by two black pawns, but again he would be perfectly safe. Black has to deal with the discovered attack, so he doesn't have time for the knight.

A third tactical trick of a knight can arise in a position where a pawn is being promoted. A knight may have the power to give check in a position where a queen would be useless.

Here is a position from a game which might have changed the course of world chess history!* Black has just played ...Rf8-f6; he threatens mate on h6. White can play d7xc8=Q, but that isn't any good because he still gets mated!
So White promotes to a knight:

d7xc8=N

Now Black doesn't have time for ... Rf6-h6 because his own king has been attacked. Mated in fact!

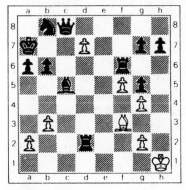

White to move

*See J.N. Walker: *Attacking the King,* pages 5 and 6.

Remember a knight can sometimes be more useful than a queen.
A knight is often able to deliver checkmate. Unlike the queen, rook, and
bishop, the knight doesn't attack a row of squares. He can only pick out
individual target squares, and this cuts down his chances of checkmating.

Even so, there are a few standard
positions where the knight proves
a winner:

Here he gets a helping hand from
the rook.

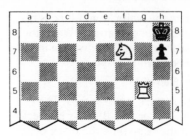

And here he has invaded the holes
around the castled position. (A
knight on e7 would also mate.)

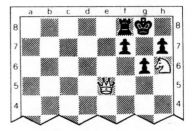

The smothered mate is a more spectacular knight mate. In this the knight
catches a king who is trapped, unable to move, because his own army is
in his way.

Sometimes it is possible to set up a
smothered mate in the opening,
before one side has developed his
pieces:

1 e2-e4	c7-c6
2 d2-d4	d7-d5
3 Nb1-c3	d5xe4
4 Nc3xe4	Nb8-d7
5 Qd1-e2	Ng8-f6
6 Ne4-d6 mate	

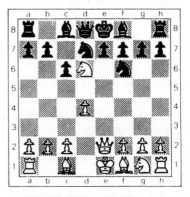

Position after 6 Ne4-d6 mate

Surrounded by his own pieces the black king was buried alive. Now he's
buried dead! The black pieces, far from giving cover to their monarch,

have completely smothered him. The white knight has raided the enemy position and used his power of jumping over the defenders to stab the king at close range.

A smothered mate is more likely to occur later in the game, when a castled king is caught in the corner.

Here the black king has been driven into the corner. His rook and pawns surround him. The white knight has hopped in and the king once again is dead and buried.

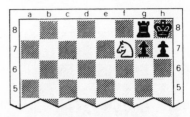

Two knights raiding as a team can combine to attack a small area with devastating effect. A single knight can attack squares of only one colour; two knights can attack both light and dark squares.

On their own two knights will not be able to force checkmate. They will either need the help of other pieces or they will have to make use of the smothering effect of enemy defenders.

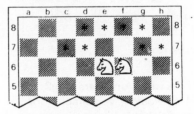

The three diagrams show just how many squares in a small section of the board can be blitzed by a pair of knights.

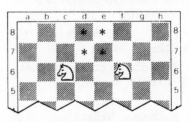

In the danger area in each of the diagrams a black king could still find escape squares. But imagine more attacking pieces in the area, imagine black defenders standing on some of those escape squares! It isn't difficult to see that a black king could be in grave danger.

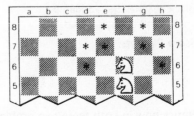

TEST ELEVEN

Four problems to solve

Q *How does Black make use of a knight fork to reach a winning endgame?*

Q *How does White make use of his well-placed knight?*

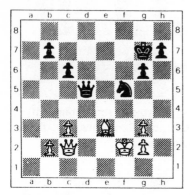

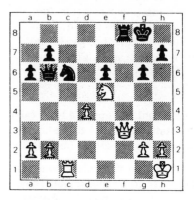

Black to move

White to move

If the white king were on g2, Black would have a simple fork on e3. Black's solution is to put the white king on g2!

| 1 ... | Qd5xg2+ |
| 2 Kf2xg2 | |

If White doesn't capture he loses his queen for nothing.

| 2 ... | Nf5xe3+ |
| 3 K moves | Ne3xc2 |

Black reaches the endgame a knight and a pawn ahead.

Score 2 points.

A fork on d7 is coming up. First White must solve the problem of his queen.

1 Qf3xf8+

White captures the rook and sets up the black king ready for the fork.

| 1 ... | Kg8xf8 |

Now White is ready.

| 2 Ne5-d7+ | K moves |
| 3 Nd7xb6 | |

The black queen falls, and White comes out of the combination a rook ahead.

Score 3 points.

Notice how in both these two problems the attacker, spotting the possible fork, drives his opponent's pieces onto the squares where he wants them.

Q *White seems to have the attack, but the knight helps Black to strike first. How?*

Q *White's knights are beautifully placed. How do they combine to force checkmate?*

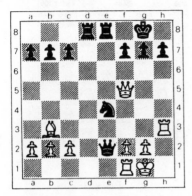

Black to move

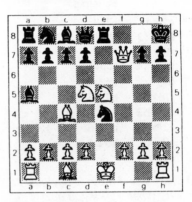

White to move

Black invades the back rank.

1	...	Qe2xf1+
2	Kg1xf1	Ne4-d2+
3	Kf1-g1	Re8-e1+
4	Kg1-h2	

Now the knight gets to work. . .

| 4 | ... | Nd2-f1+ |

The white king must come back on to the first rank. . .

| 5 | Kh2-g1 | |

. . .and now the black knight can discover check.

| 5 | ... | Nf1-g3+ |

Discovering check on e3 is just as good. Either way the knight cannot be captured; so Black regains his queen and remains a rook ahead.

Score 5 points.

The black king is cornered and White makes use of the threat of smothered mate.

| 1 | Qf7-g8+ | Kh8xg8 |

If Black captures with the rook he smothers his king, and White mates with his knight on f7.

| 2 | Nd5-e7++ | |

Double check!

| 2 | ... | Kg8-f8 |

The black king would love to run back into his corner, but 2 . . . Kg8-h8 3 Ne5-f7 is mate. Useful knights!

| 3 | Ne5-g6+ | h7xg6 |
| 4 | Ne7xg6 mate | |

The bishop holds the light squares, the knight holds the dark squares. The black king is caught in the net.

Score 5 points.

Testgame 11

(*Ruy López*)

	Pegoraro	Scheipel
1	e2-e4	e7-e5
2	Ng1-f3	Nb8-c6
3	Bf1-b5	a7-a6
4	Bb5-a4	Ng8-f6
5	0-0	Bf8-e7
6	Qd1-e2	b7-b5
7	Ba4-b3	0-0
8	c2-c3	d7-d6
9	a2-a4	b5-b4
10	c3xb4	

Q *Black's next move is obvious. . . or is it? What would you do?*

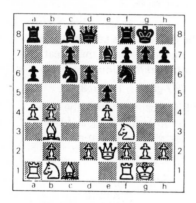

10 ...   Bc8-g4!

Score 4 points.

With his last move White left himself with a whacking great hole on d4, and a black knight is already in position to home in.

Score 2 points for the obvious 10 . . .Nc6xb4.

11 Qe2-c4

Q *What does Black do now?*

11 ...   Bg4xf3

Score 3 points.

Black destroys White's knight and prepares to occupy d4 with his own.

Score 1 point for 11 . . .Qd8-d7.

12 g2xf3

Naturally White didn't like 12 Qc4xc6 Bf3xe4 when he loses a valuable centre pawn.

12 ...   Nc6-d4

Of course! The knight seizes the splendid outpost.

White's problems are clear:

(a) The black knight dominates the centre and he can't do anything about it. He can't kick the knight out with a pawn, and it's going to take him ages to bring a piece round to threaten it.

(b) His castled position is shattered, his king is in danger on an open file, and his pawns on f3 and h2 are obvious weaknesses.

(c) He is behind in development, and those pieces that are in play are too far away to help their king.

(d) His pawns on f2 and f3 form a nuisance barrier. They stop his king fleeing for safety to the centre; they also stop his pieces from coming to the aid of his king.

13 Bb3-d1

Q *What does Black do to strengthen his position?*

13 ... Nf6-h5

Score 4 points.
The battle will be fought on the K-side of the board — mainly around the white king. Black must mobilize his forces and bring them to the scene of the action before White has time to sort out his mess and organize a defence. One black knight is already installed on an excellent base; the second picks his spot: f4.

Score 2 points for 13 . . .Qd8-d7.

14 d2-d3

Q *What is Black's next move?*

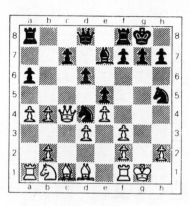

14 ... Be7-g5!

Score 4 points.
White's dark-squared bishop guards f4. Black's dark-squared bishop only gets in the way of his own queen. The solution is to exchange them!

Score 1 point for 14 . . .Qd8-d7.
Lose 2 points for 14 . . .Nh5-f4 which loses a piece because the black e-pawn is overloaded defending both knights.

15 Kg1-h1 Bg5-f4

Black's first target is h2. He threatens 16 . . .Qd8-h4 and mate next move.

16 Bc1xf4 Nh5xf4

The second knight digs in. With White's dark-squared bishop gone Black's hold over his operation bases, f4 and d4, is even stronger.

17 Rf1-g1

White has grovelled to guard g2 against invasion by the black queen. Now he has left f2 as a target.

Q *How should Black continue his build-up?*

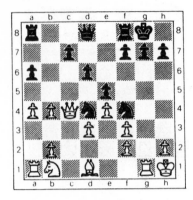

17 ...   Nf4-h3

Score 4 points.

The knight begins its raiding and f2 comes under fire.

Score 1 point for 17 ...Qd8-h4.

18 Rg1-g2   Qd8-h4

The queen joins the attack and the pawn on f2 falls immediately. The white pieces are helpless. The black knight radiates power from d4. He cuts White in two. By blocking the pawn on d3 and hitting c2, he stops the white queen from coming to the rescue.

19 Nb1-d2

If 19 Qc4xc7, Black grabs the open c-file by 19 ...Ra8-c8 and soon invades the back rank.

19 ...   Nh3xf2+
20 Kh1-g1   Nf2-h3+
21 Kg1-f1   Nh3-f4

The knight returns to Camp III: he doesn't want to be stuck on the edge of the board.

22 Rg2-f2   Qh4-h3+

Q *Is it safe for the white king to run away to the centre by 23 Kf1-e1?*

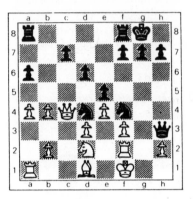

No. After 23 Kf1-e1 Nf4-g2+, White will have to give up the exchange, since 24 Ke1-f1 Ng2-e3++ is a most horrible fork.

Score 3 points if you saw this.

23 Kf1-g1

Q *Now what should Black do?*

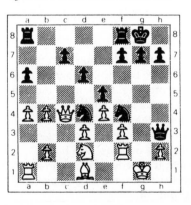

23 ...   Ra8-e8

Score 3 points.

The first stage of Black's attack has come to a halt. Reinforcements are needed.

Score 1 point for 23 . . .Rf8-e8. Black's king's position is safer if he keeps a rook on f8.

24	Nd2-f1	Re8-e6
25	Nf1-e3	Re6-g6+
26	Kg1-h1	Rg6-g3!

Black nets the pawn on f3, but his real plan is to force the exchange of rooks after which the white king will be open to the wind.

27 Ra1-c1   Nd4xf3

At last the queen's knight springs from his base. Even now White can't get rid of him! If 28 Bd1xf3 Rg3xf3, and White can choose between losing his own knight and being mated.

28 Bd1-b3

Q *How does Black continue the attack?*

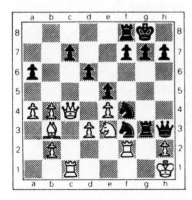

28 . . .   Rg3-g2!
Score 5 points.

Black threatens mate on h2, and so forces the exchange of rooks.

29 Rf2xg2   Nf4xg2

White still can't capture on g2 with his knight. He must save the knight and defend h2.

30 Ne3-f1

Q *How does Black finish White off?*

30 . . .   Ng2-e3!!

Splat!

Score 5 points.

Glorious, glorious knights! They hit everything in sight; g2, h2, the white queen, c2, the white knight. . . At this point not surprisingly White resigned.

You could hardly have a better example of knights operating from bases. Both black knights dug themselves in on squares from which they could not be removed. The king's knight raided the weaknesses in White's ruined castled position. The queen's knight just sat still, a giant, commanding the board. Together they were a frightening force that White could never stop.

The glory of André Philidor

Born near Paris in 1726, André-Francois-Danican Philidor was the greatest chess-player the world had yet known. At only fourteen he took on and beat all the leading players at the Café de la Régence in Paris, looked upon as the centre of world chess. He toured Europe and defeated everyone who offered him a challenge. At only twenty he published *An Analysis of Chess,* the first ever really good guide to chess strategy. Philidor's book was a best-seller in its day; now it is forgotten. Philidor is remembered today for two things. First there is *Philidor's Defence,* the opening which begins 1 e2-e4 e7-e5 2 Ng1-f3 d7-d6. Then there is *Philidor's Legacy,* a smothered mating method which has cropped up in countless games. Every chess-player should know *Philidor's Legacy.*

Start with this position. White forces the black king into the corner:

1 Qc6-e6+   Kg8-h8

If the king ever goes to f8 he is mated by the white queen on f7.

2 Ne5-f7+   Kh8-g8
3 Nf7-h6++   Kg8-h8
4 Qe6-g8+!   Rb8xg8

Forced! But now his king is trapped.

5 Nh6-f7 mate

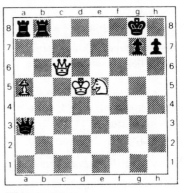

White to move

Philidor's Legacy. . .the smothered mate. . .the discovery Philidor left for the world of chess. Bravo Philidor! But. . . the position above is taken from a book called *A Discourse of Love and the Art of Chess,* by the Spanish player Lucena. That book was published in 1497 — two hundred and twenty-nine years before Philidor was even born! Philidor deserves his glory, he rightly holds an important position in the history of chess, but history has given him the credit for somebody else's idea. Oh, and by the way, André-Francois-Danican Philidor. . .he never played Philidor's Defence in his life!

Death by suffocation

A smothered attack often brings a sudden, shock ending to a game; it is very easy to miss.

Sudden? Well, a smothered attack brought an end to the shortest game ever decided between two players of master standard. Here is that game, from the Paris Championship of 1924:

(*Queen's Pawn Game*)

Gibaud	Lazard
1 d2-d4	Ng8-f6
2 Nb1-d2	e7-e5
3 d4xe5	Nf6-g4
4 h2-h3	Ng4-e3!
5 White resigns	

Gibaud's queen has just died; smothered in her bed! (5 f2xe3 Qd8-h4+ mates.)

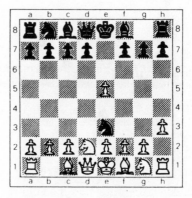

Position after 4 . . .Ng4-e3

Shock? Well, four allies got one in 1936. They sat down to play black together against World Champion Alexander Alekhine. After **1 e2-e4 c7-c6 2 d2-d4 d7-d5 3 Nb1-c3 d5xe4 4 Nc3xe4 Nb8-d7 5 Qd1-e2**, they played **5 . . . Ng8-f6**. Obviously they had not read page 102!

Easy to miss? Well, ask our old friend Dufresne — you remember, the one who wished he hadn't accepted all of Anderssen's presents.

Dufresne, together with Jacques Mieses, wrote *The Book of Chess-play.* And a very good book it was too, being printed and reprinted many times. In the eighth edition they analysed the Queen's Gambit Opening. After Black's ninth move they reached this position. 'Black has the better position', they said. Quite right. . .unless White just happens to notice that he can play 10 Nb5-d6 mate!

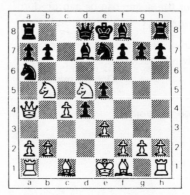

Position after 9 . . .Ng8-e7

TEST TWELVE

Four problems to solve

Q *The black knight can discover check in eight different ways. Which is the right way?*

Q *Both black knights help in finishing White off quickly. How does Black set up the winning forks?*

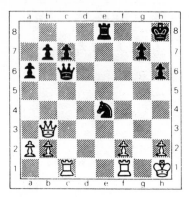

Black to move

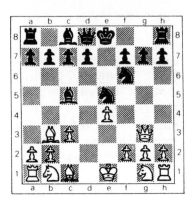

Black to move

Discovering check gives the knight a chance to invade the white king's position.

1 ...   Ne4-g3++

Double check! Neither the knight nor the queen can be captured.

2 Kh1-g1

Now Black has two methods of giving checkmate:

2 ...   Qc6-h1 mate, or
2 ...   Ng3-e2 mate

Score 2 points.

Black drags a white piece on to f2 and into a knight fork.

1 ...   Bc5xf2+

His king and queen are forked by the bishop; so White must capture. He has a choice: (a) 2 Ke1xf2 or (b) 2 Qg3xf2.

(a)
2 Ke1xf2   Nf6xe4+

...and White has walked smack into a knight fork.

(b)
2 Qg3xf2   Ne5-d3+

...and White has walked smack into a knight fork!

Score 3 points.

Q *Black has more pieces. He threatens . . .Rf5-f1 mate and . . . Rg8xg4. White gets the winning position! How?*

Q *White has destroyed Black's K-side pawn shield. How does he invade and finish off the enemy king?*

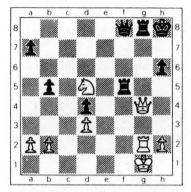

White to move

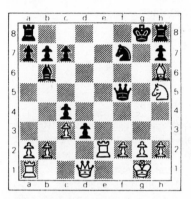

White to move

White spots the possibility of a knight fork on e7. He has to set it up by driving the black pieces where he wants them.

1 Qg4xg8+   Qf8xg8
2 Rg2xg8+   Kh8xg8

Now the black pieces are on the right squares and White can go ahead with his fork.

3 Nd5-e7+   K moves
4 Ne7xf5

White is a piece ahead and wins the ending easily.

Score 4 points.

White notices that Nh5-f6+ would be mate if it were not for the black queen. So, he sets about the job of deflecting her.

1 Re2-e8+

White makes way for his queen to come into the attack.

1 . . .   Ra8xe8
2 Qd1-g4+   Qf5xg4

The black queen is dragged away from f6, but blocking the check is no good either:

(a) 2 . . .Qf5-g5 3 Nh5-f6 mate, or (b) 2 . . .Nf7-g5 3 Qg4xf5 winning the queen.

3 Nh5-f6 mate

Score 6 points.

Testgame 12

(Sicilian Defence — Morra Gambit)

1	e2-e4	c7-c5
2	d2-d4	c5xd4
3	c2-c3	

White offers a pawn. . .

3	. . .	d4xc3

. . .and Black accepts.

4 Nb1xc3

For the pawn sacrificed White will gain compensation in three ways:

(a) He will have a small lead in development.

(b) He will have open lines: the c- and d-files, plus good diagonals for his bishops.

(c) He will have more space in the centre of the board.

4	. . .	Nb8-c6
5	Ng1-f3	Ng8-f6

Q *What is White's next developing move?*

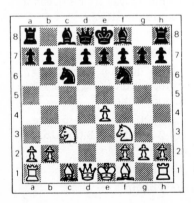

6 Bf1-c4

Score 3 points.

The best diagonal: the bishop hits the weak point at f7. White must work hard to make use of his advantages and keep Black under pressure. He must not allow his opponent time to complete his development and hold on to his extra pawn.

Score 1 point for 6 Bc1-f4 or 6 Bc1-g5.

6	. . .	d7-d6?
7	e4-e5	

White presses on.

7	. . .	d6xe5

He can't play 7 . . .Nc6xe5 8 Nf3xe5 d6xe5 9 Bc4xf7+ since he will lose his queen.

Q *What does White do now?*

8 Qd1xd8+!

Score 4 points.

The only way of keeping up the pressure. It may seem strange that White should want to exchange queens after giving up two pawns to get an attack. Exchanges usually help the player whose position is cramped, but they can also help the player who has a lead in development. Here the white knights are ready to rip Black apart, and the black pieces are in no position to meet them.

8 ...   Nc6xd8

Taking with the king is even worse!
8...Ke8xd8 9 Nf3-g5 (threatening a fork on f7) Kd8-e8 10 Nc3-b5 (threatening a fork on c7!)

Q *How does White continue with his attack?*

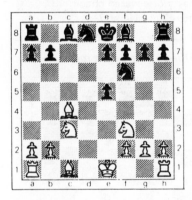

9 Nc3-b5

Score 4 points.
The raiding begins; the first knight hits c7 with the threat of a fork.

Score 1 point for 9 Nf3xe5.

9 ...   Ra8-b8

Black doesn't have much choice. He still gets forked after 9...Nd8-e6 10 Bc4xe6, and if he tries 9...Ke8-d7 10 Nf3xe5+ Kd7-e8 the knight goes to c7 anyway — only now it mates him!

Q *How should White continue?*

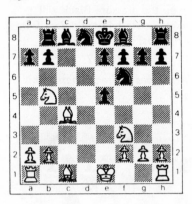

10 Nf3xe5

Score 4 points.
The second knight goes to war!
Mate is threatened on c7.
No score for 10 Nb5xa7. White is after more than getting back his pawns.

10 ...   e7-e6

Q *What is the next attacking move?*

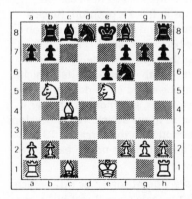

11 Nb5-c7+

Score 3 points.

The only move. If White doesn't keep up the pressure Black will play 11...Bf8-b4+ and 12...0-0, solving most of his problems.

11 ... Ke8-e7

Q *How does White strengthen his attack?*

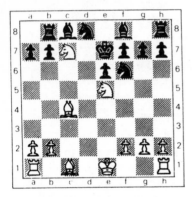

12 Bc1-e3

Score 4 points.
The white knights have caused chaos in Black's position. Black's pieces stand higgledy-piggledy on the back rank, and his king, having lost the right to castle, is stuck firmly in the centre. White's knights can't be expected to do everything themselves, and more fire-power is needed in the attack. White develops a bishop with the threat of 13 Be3-c5 mate: Black is not to be allowed any peace.

Score 1 point for 12 Bc1-d2, which has the same mate threat but blocks the d-file.

Score 1 point for 12 b2-b3 or 12 Bc1-f4.

12 ... Ke7-d6

The black king runs for his life and forks the two white knights. On the open board the knights lack pawn support; so they have no safe operation bases. They must expect to fight a hit-and-run battle, but now they have a problem...they can't both run away! White has an answer ready...

13 Be3-f4

Now if the black king captures the knight on c7 he walks straight into a nasty discovered check: 13...Kd6xc7 14 Ne5xf7+.

13 ... Nf6-h5

Q *Find White's next move.*

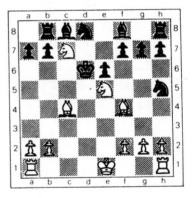

14 Nc7-b5+

Score 4 points.
White saves his knight, and as he gives check he doesn't lose time — he keeps the attack rolling.

Score 1 point for 14 Ne5xf7++. Discovering check isn't so good now, because after 14...Kd6-e7 15 Nf7xh8 Nh5xf4, White hasn't a hope of rescuing his knight.

Q *What would White do if Black dived for safety by playing 14 ...Kd6-e7?*

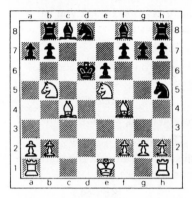

The black king is on the run and White is hunting him down. The white pieces will form the spider's web, drawing the black king in until he is securely trapped.

15	...	Kc5-b4
16	a2-a3+	Kb4-a4
17	b2-b3+	Ka4-a5
18	b3-b4+	Bf8xb4+

Black gets mated immediately if he moves his king: 18 ...Ka5-a6 19 Nb5-c7 mate or 18 ...Ka5-a4 19 Nb5-c3 mate.

19 a3xb4++ Ka5xb4

Q *What does White do now?*

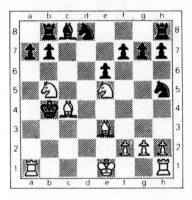

After 14 ...Kd6-e7 White would be able to use his knight for another discovered attack: 15 Ne5-g6+ followed by 16 Bf4xb8.
Score 3 points if you saw this.

14 ... Kd6-c5

Q *The black king is a target for White's army. What does White do now?*

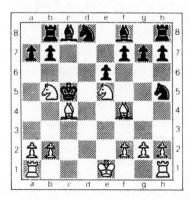

15 Bf4-e3+
Score 3 points.

20 0-0
Score 3 points.
The black king has been netted by White's minor pieces. He can only sit and await execution by 21 Rf1-b1.
Score 3 points for 20 Ke1-d2, but *score only 1 point* for 20 Ke1-e2 which allows Black to delay mate by 20 ...Nh5-f4+.

Black resigns

Raiding knights at their best!

Come into my parlour said the spider to the fly

Black seems to be winning fairly easily. He's got the white pieces squashed into the corner, and he has more than enough threats to keep anyone happy.

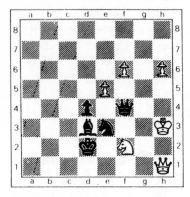

White to move

White, of course, has different ideas, or at least his queen does! She notices that if she can entice the black king on to the right square (e1, c1, b2, b4, or c5), she can clobber him with a real killer of a knight fork.

1 Qh1-e1+

Hello then Handsome.

1 . . .   Kd2-c2

I beg your pardon Madam?

2 Qe1-c1+

I said Hello then Handsome.

2 . . .   Kc2-b3

Strange woman. . .Go away.

3 Qc1-b2+

Now then, don't be shy. . .come here.

3 . . .   Kb3-c4

Really Madam, I think you've made a mistake.

4 Qb2-b4+

Oh come on now, how about a dance?

4 . . .   Kc4-d5

Do you mind, Madam. I think not.

5 Qb4-d6+

Oh yes. . .take me in those strong arms.

5 . . .   Kd5-c4

Madam, please. . .

6 Qd6-c5+

Hold me closer. . .tighter. . .tighter.

6 . . .   Kc4-b3

Madam please. . .put me down.

7 Qc5-b4+

Oh you're mine. . .mine.

7 . . .   Kb3-c2

Control yourself Madam. Your lipstick's smudging all over my royal uniform.

8 Qb4-b2+

At last. . .there is no escape. I am yours. . .all yours.

8 . . .   Kc2xb2

Oh the woman's raving mad!

9 Nf2xd3+

The white queen has finally got her man! The black king, forced to surrender to her feminine wiles, gets horribly forked. The white passed pawns march on to victory.

Von Schierstedt at odds with a knight

In the last century games were often played at odds. There weren't so
many good players about, and smashing the same opponents night after
night can be as boring for the chess master as it is miserable for his victims.
So they invented games which gave the weaker player a chance. Often
they played *odds games,* in which the master gave his opponent a piece, a
rook, or even a queen start. Less common was the game in which the
master had to name before the first move the piece with which he intended to give checkmate. Doing this you will find, if you dare try, isn't
easy! Max Lange dared. In Breslau in 1868 he undertook to beat von
Schierstedt. . .by mating him with his queen's knight, of all pieces!

(*Vienna Gambit*)

	Lange	von Schierstedt
1	e2-e4	e7-e5
2	Nb1-c3	Nb8-c6
3	f2-f4	e5xf4
4	Ng1-f3	g7-g5
5	Bf1-c4	g5-g4
6	0-0	

A piece, for development.

6	. . .	g4xf3
7	d2-d4	f3xg2
8	Bc4xf7+	

A piece, to get at the enemy king.

8	. . .	Ke8xf7
9	Qd1-h5+	Kf7-g7
10	Rf1xf4	

Threatening mate on f7 though
not with the knight.

10	. . .	Ng8-h6
11	Bc1-e3	d7-d6
12	Nc3-e2	Qd8-e7
13	Kg1xg2	Bc8-e6
14	Ra1-f1	Be6-f7

15	Qh5xh6+	Kg7xh6
16	Rf4-g4+	Kh6-h5
17	Ne2-g3+	Kh5xg4
18	Rf1-f5	h7-h6
19	h2-h3+	Kg4-h4
20	Rf5-h5+	Bf7xh5
21	Ng3-f5 mate	

The queen's knight wins the day. . .
not that Lange had much choice —
he didn't have much else left!

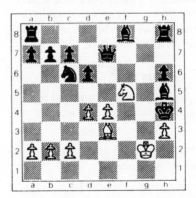

A brilliant attack. . .but if Lange could only win by checkmating with his
queen's knight, why didn't von Schierstedt makes some attempt to exchange that piece? And why did he bother defending himself when Lange
threatened mate with his rook?

TEST THIRTEEN

Four problems to solve

Q *Black wins a piece by means of a simple fork. How?*

Q *Black's pieces are moving in for the kill. How does he force checkmate?*

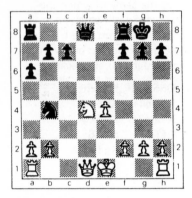

Black to move

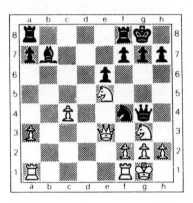

Black to move

Black spots the chance of a knight fork on c2. He can't go there straight away, so he sets up the fork with a queen sacrifice.

1 ...   Qd8xd4

2 Qd1xd4

If White had not recaptured he would simply have lost a piece.

2 ...   Nb4-c2+

The knight forks everything — king, queen, and rook!

3 K moves   Nc2xd4

Black has regained the queen and come out a knight up.

Score 2 points.

If the white g-pawn disappears, Black has a standard knight mate on h3.

1 ...   Qg4-h3

Black threatens mate on g2 and invites White to move that g-pawn.

2 g2xh3

The pawn is lured away and the path is open for the knight.

2 ...   Nf4xh3 mate

Score 3 points.

Q *Black is a piece ahead; White must strike quickly. How?*

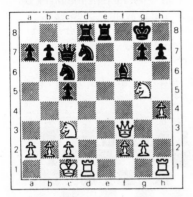

White to move

Q *The white knight deals the death blows. How?*

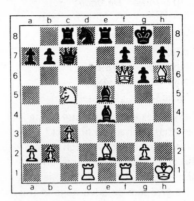

White to move

The white knight on g5 holds the key to the attack. White forces mate by a standard Philidor's Legacy.

1 Qf3-d5+   Kg8-h8

Or 1 . . .Kg8-f8 2 Qd5-f7 mate.

2 Ng5-f7+   Kh8-g8
3 Nf7-h6++

Double check; the knight can't be taken.

3 . . .   Kg8-h8

Again 3 . . .Kg8-f8 4 Qd5-f7 is mate.

4 Qd5-g8+   Re8xg8
5 Nh6-f7 mate

The black king is smothered in the corner in the familiar way.

Score 4 points.

White sparks off a series of murderous forks.

1 Nc5xe4

Score 3 points for this fine queen sacrifice.

1 . . .   Be5xf6

Otherwise Black has simply lost a piece for nothing.

2 Ne4xf6+

The first fork.

2 . . .   Kg8-h8

White could now win by 3 Nf6xe8, but he sets up an even better fork.

3 Bh6-g7+

Score 3 more points if you saw this second sacrifice.

3 . . .   Kh8xg7
4 Nf6xe8+   K moves
5 Ne8xc7

White has won a rook and a bishop!

Testgame 13

(*Nimzo-Indian Defence*)
H. Mattison   A. Nimzowitsch

1	d2-d4	Ng8-f6
2	c2-c4	e7-e6
3	Nb1-c3	Bf8-b4
4	Ng1-f3	Bb4xc3+
5	b2xc3	

The game is already taking shape. Black has exchanged his dark-squared bishop for a knight. If White can exchange pawns, and open up diagonals, his two bishops could give him an advantage in the middle-game.

On the other hand White's pawn structure has been seriously weakened. The white c-pawns are doubled; they will have to be defended by pieces, and the one on c4 is going to get in the way of his own bishop. The white a-pawn is isolated.

Black must fight for his share of the centre, but he must not allow the pawn exchanges which will let the white bishops loose on an open board. He must try to keep the position closed and look for ways to attack the white pawn weaknesses.

5	...	d7-d6
6	Qd1-c2	

White wants to push his e-pawn all the way to e5, seizing space, annoying the black knight, and opening up diagonals for his bishops.

6	...	Qd8-e7

Black plans to answer e2-e4 with . . . e6-e5, staking his own claim for space in the centre.

7	Bc1-a3

With this move White has two ideas in mind. First he pins the black d-pawn and prevents . . .e6-e5. Second he prepares to get rid of his doubled pawns by playing c4-c5.

Q *How does Black stop White's plan?*

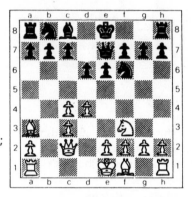

7	...	c7-c5!

Score 5 points.
Black sets up a road-block. This pawn blunts the white bishop, and fixes the white pawn firmly on c4 where it will soon be attacked.

8	g2-g3	b7-b6
9	Bf1-g2	Bc8-b7
10	0-0	0-0
11	Nf3-h4?	

Knights are usually badly placed on the edge of the board, and this one is badly placed here! If White wanted to exchange the bishops then he should have played his knight back to d2, where it defends the c-pawn and helps control the centre.

11 ...   Bb7xg2
12 Kg1xg2

Here again White should have
taken with the knight so that it
could get back into the game on e3.

12 ...   Qe7-b7+
13 Kg2-g1   Qb7-a6

c4 is the obvious target, and the
attack begins. White's reply is
forced...

14 Qc2-b3

...but now he loses control of e4.

Q *What does Black do now?*

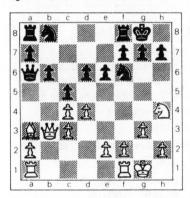

14 ...   Nb8-c6

Score 3 points.
Black has played the opening well.
He has kept up in development and
he has more than his share of the
centre. He has stopped the white
bishops from controlling the board
by setting up his solid pawn barrier.
The middle-game is not going to be
won by a violent attack on the white
king. Black is going to gradually improve the position of his pieces and
attack the weak points in White's
pawn structure.

15 Rf1-d1

Q *How does Black continue his
build-up?*

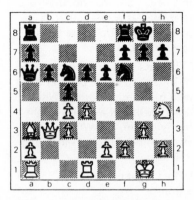

15 ...   Nc6-a5

Score 4 points.
Knights are usually badly placed on
the edge of the board...but not always! This one hits c4 as well as
the queen.

16 Qb3-b5   Qa6xb5
17 c4xb5

Q *What does Black do now to
strengthen his position?*

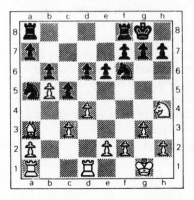

17 . . .   Na5-c4!

Score 6 points.

Black has captured c4! He hasn't won a pawn, but that doesn't matter. He has won a square, a marvellous operation base for his knight. Just look:

(a) The base is a stronghold. It is a light square, so White can't attack it with his bishop. Nor can White attack it with a pawn. The knight is firmly dug in, and White will have enormous problems in trying to shift it.

(b) The knight commands a central position.

(c) The white bishop is attacked and driven back home.

(d) The dark squares which the bishop might like to use are attacked.

(e) The white pawn is blocked and fixed on c3 where it will both get in the way of its bishop and be a target for attack.

(f) The black pawns on d6 and b6 are protected by the knight.

Score 2 points for 17 . . .Nf6-d5 or 17 . . .Nf6-e4. Sooner or later one of these squares is going to be an ideal base for the king's knight. However, if Black uses either of them immediately White would simply defend his c-pawn by **18 Rd1-d3** and then grab the first opportunity to drive the knight off with a pawn.

18 Ba3-c1

Q *What does Black do now to improve the power of his pieces?*

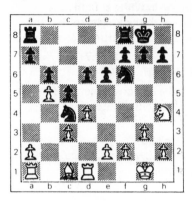

18 . . .   a7-a6!

Score 5 points.

The time has come for Black to think about his rooks. Rooks need open files. Black opens a file and finds a new target — the white pawn on a2.

Score 1 point for 18 . . . Nf6-d5 or 18 . . . Nf6-e4.

19 b5xa6   Ra8xa6
20 d4xc5   b6xc5
21 Nh4-g2

Q *What does Black do now?*

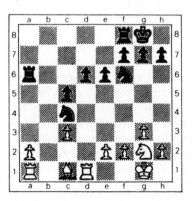

21 ...   Nf6-d5

Score 4 points.
The second knight finds a base
from which to operate. He stands
smack in the middle of the board,
on a light square where the bishop
can't get at him, and he hits the
weak white c-pawn.
Score 2 points for 21 ...Rf8-a8.
Score 1 point for 21 ...Nf6-e4.

22 Rd1-d3

Q *How does Black keep up the
pressure?*

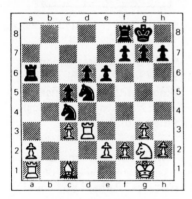

22 ...   Rf8-a8

Score 4 points.
Black has steadily improved the
position of his pieces and com-
pared with White's ragged army
they make a splendid sight. Black
has secured operation bases for his
knights. He has created open files
for his rooks. He has positioned his
forces to work together powerfully.
Now it is harvest time! The weak
white pawns are over-ripe, ready
to fall.
Score 2 points for 22 ...Nc4-e5.

23 e2-e4

Q *What should Black play now?*

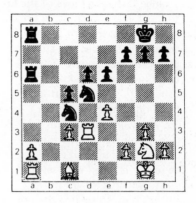

23 ...   Nc4-e5

Score 4 points.
Score 2 points for 23 ...Nd5-f6.
The magnificent knights stand
astride the board. They simply
radiate power. So much power, in
fact, that Mattison, who has not yet
lost so much as a pawn, gave up.
White resigned.
Why?
Well, if he had played on Mattison
would have had to try:

24 Rd3-d1
If 24 Rd3-d2, he gets forked by 24
...Ne5-f3+.

24 ...   Nd5xc3
25 Rd1-f1
He can't go to d2 or e1 because of
the fork.

25 ...   Ne5-f3+
26 Kg1-h1   Ra6xa2

And now, having already surren-
dered two pawns, White has no way
of saving a third, his e-pawn.

The knight move

The strange L-shaped move of the knight has interested people for hundreds of years, in chess, in life, and in stories. In the Middle Ages secret messages were sent in code, by knight moves. A sheet of paper was covered in squares and a letter was placed in each square. The reader by moving like a knight from square to square could spell out the hidden message. In our picture you will find a useful message if you start in the top left corner. Of course, at each go the reader is faced with several squares to which a knight move

K	Z	Q	N	X	F
Y	P	H	E	R	I
E	E	K	G	T	H
T	Z	O	D	P	U
S	E	Y	F	H	G
Q	F	T	E	O	B

would take him, so solving the problem often took both time and patience.

The German High Command, in the Russian film *Blue Routes,* cunningly designed a minefield where 36 mines were linked together in the pattern of knight moves. Of course the Germans reckoned without the super-brain of Comrade Captain Ratanov of the Soviet Navy, who saw through the whole evil plot in a flash, and destroyed the lot of them!

The knight's tour of the chess-board has always captured most attention. How can the knight move around the board landing on each of the 64 squares once, without touching any square twice? Perhaps you could find a way?

It isn't easy. . .but there are over 30 million methods! Here is one of them. The knight begins at d4, moves to c2, then to a1, to b3, and so on before reaching c6, its 64th and last square.

The strange thing about this knight tour is that in touring the board the knight makes a magic square. Add up the numbers in each rank and each file, you will find they always come to 260. Of course,

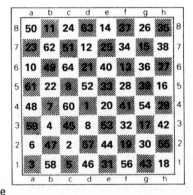

it's not a proper magic square because the diagonals don't add up to 260 as well. Perhaps you could work out a way of solving that problem . . . if you've got a year or two to spare!

The knight transfer

Here is a problem for you.
Both players have made four
moves and this is the position.
Your job is to work out the moves
they made. How can you reach
this position after just four moves?

Difficult?

Well, play through the game below
and you may get a clue!

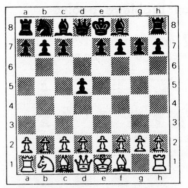

Position after Black's fourth move

Something rather strange happened in the first ten moves of the game
between Berger and Marshall at Carlsbad in 1907.

(*Centre Counter Gambit*)

1	e2-e4	d7-d5
2	e4xd5	Ng8-f6
3	Ng1-f3	Nf6xd5
4	d2-d4	e7-e6
5	Bf1-d3	Nb8-d7
6	0-0	Bf8-e7
7	c2-c4	Nd5-b4
8	Bd3-e2	0-0
9	a2-a3	Nb4-c6
10	Nb1-c3	Nd7-f6

Position after 10 . . .Nd7-f6

Nothing strange? Quite a normal position, you might think. The odd
thing is that Marshall's knights have changed places. His king's knight,
normally developed on f6, sits on c6, whilst his queen's knight, which
you would expect to find on c6, sits on f6.

If you were stuck on the problem above, that knight transfer may
have given you a hint. You see, in the problem one of the knights is not
what it seems. The solution to the problem is: **1 Ng1-f3 d7-d5 2 Nf3-e5
Ng8-f6 3 Ne5-c6 Nf6-d7 4 Nc6xb8 Nd7xb8.** The black knight on b8 is
in fact Black's king's knight!

TEST FOURTEEN

Four problems to solve

Q *The knight helps White to bring the game to a sudden end. How?*

Q *Black sets up a winning knight fork. How?*

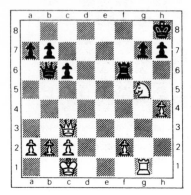

White to move

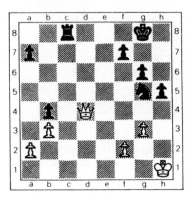

Black to move

A queen sacrifice clears the way for a standard rook-and-knight mate.

1 Qc3xf6

If Black doesn't accept the sacrifice he remains a rook and knight down — checkmate will not be far away.

1 . . .   g7xf6
2 Ng5-f7 mate

The king is neatly trapped in his corner.

Score 2 points.

The important square is f3, but before Black can fork he must drive the white king on to h2 or g1.

1 . . .   Rc8-c1+
2 Kh1-g2

Or 2 Kh1-h2 Ng5-f3+ when the king and queen are forked straight away.

2 . . .   Rc1-g1+

Black drives the king where he wants him.

3 Kg2xg1

Now the fork is set up.

3 . . .   Ng5-f3+
4 K moves   Nf3xd4

Black has won the queen for a rook. The ending, a knight and pawn ahead, is easy to win.

Score 3 points.

Q *Black's g-pawn looks menacing, but it is his knight that does the damage. What knight? Well, that is the question!*

Q *All of White's pieces are well placed. A sacrifice leads the way to a knight raid and checkmating attack. Find the way White wins.*

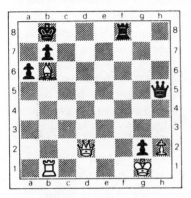

Black to move

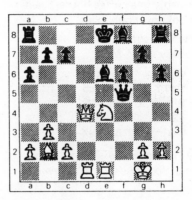

White to move

Obviously the g-pawn is going to promote to a knight. Black cleverly arranges for the knight to get an immediate fork.

1 ...   Rf8-f1+
2 Rb1xf1   Qh5xh2+
3 Kg1xh2

If the king tries to run away he only gets into greater trouble: 3 Kg1-f2 g2xf1=Q+ 4 Kf2xf1 Qh2xd2.

3 ...   g2xf1=N+

Black promotes to a knight and White finds he has walked into a real beauty of a fork!

4 K moves   Nf1xd2

Black, with two extra pawns, wins the endgame quite easily.

Score 4 points.

White's strength is on the open centre files. He makes use of these files with a couple of deadly discovered checks.

1 Qd4-d7+

The queen is sacrificed to help clear the e-file.

1 ...   Be6xd7
2 Ne4-d6++

The knight raids deep into enemy territory, discovering check.

2 ...   Ke8-d8
3 Nd6-f7+   Kd8-c8
4 Re1-e8+

The rook is sacrificed, this time to help clear the d-file.

4 ...   Bd7xe8
5 Rd1-d8 mate

Score 6 points.

Testgame 14

This is a superb little game by Paul Morphy, played in Paris in 1859, probably in a coffee house, against an unknown opponent.

(*Two Knights Defence*)

Morphy	Mr ?
1 e2-e4	e7-e5
2 Ng1-f3	Nb8-c6
3 Bf1-c4	Ng8-f6
4 d2-d4	e5xd4
5 0-0	Nf6xe4

Q *Two pawns down, how does White continue with his opening plan?*

6 Rf1-e1

Score 3 points.
The immediate problem facing Black is the open e-file. His king is stuck on the end of it, and his knight is loose, a target in midboard. White seizes the open file and puts Black under pressure straight away.

Score 2 points for 6 Nb1-c3. This leads to wild positions after 6 . . . d4xc3 7 Bc4xf7+ Ke8xf7 8 Qd1-d5+, but leaves White with little hope of an advantage if Black plays 6 . . . Ne4xc3.

Score 1 point for 6 Nf3xd4. This regains one of the pawns but doesn't put Black under any pressure, giving him the chance to complete his development. The black pawn on d4 isn't going to run away, so White need not be in any hurry to recapture.

6 . . .	d7-d5
7 Bc4xd5	Qd8xd5

Q *How does White regain his piece?*

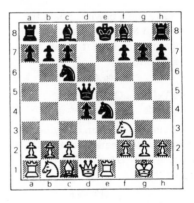

8 Nb1-c3!

Score 4 points.
White makes excellent use of the fact that both Black's knight and his d-pawn are pinned along the centre files. He develops a piece, forking Black's queen and knight.

8 ...   Qd5-h5
9 Nc3xe4

Threatening a deadly discovered check.

9 ...   Bc8-e6

Black shuts the file.

10 Ne4-g5   Bf8-b4

Q *What should White do now?*

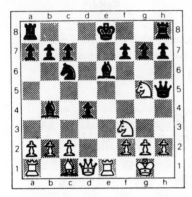

11 Re1xe6+!

Score 6 points.

Black was beginning to solve his problems. His pieces were taking up good positions and his king was about to escape from the centre. This sacrifice rocks Black right back on his heels. White solves his problem of what to do with his rook, and at the same time anchors the black king where he wants him.

Score 2 points for 11 Re1-e4.
Score 1 point for 11 Bc1-d2.

11 ...   f7xe6
12 Ng5xe6

The knight seizes a magnificent post, hitting four vital squares. He threatens forks on g7 and c7, and

he stops Black castling by attacking d8 and f8. The black king is now stranded firmly in the centre.

12 ...   Qh5-f7

Q *How should White continue the attack?*

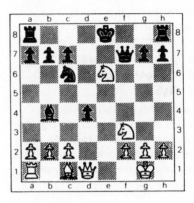

13 Nf3-g5

Score 4 points.
The second knight joins the attack.

Score 2 points for 13 Qd1-e2,
threatening to discover check.

13 ...   Qf7-e7
14 Qd1-e2   Bb4-d6

Q *Now what should White play?*

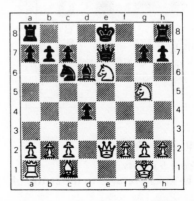

15 Ne6xg7+

Score 3 points.
White makes use of the pin on the open e-file to allow his knight to raid further into enemy territory. Without pawn support there is very little chance of the white knights being able to dig themselves in on safe operation bases; they must fight a hit-and-run battle.

15 . . .   Ke8-d7
16 Qe2-g4+ Kd7-d8
17 Ng5-f7+

The knights combine with murderous effect. White could equally well have played 17 Ng5-e6+ when Black would have had to march his king straight into a discovered check.

17 . . .   Qe7xf7
18 Bc1-g5+ Bd6-e7

Q *How does White keep up the pressure?*

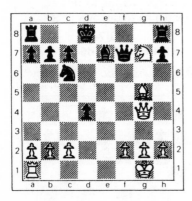

19 Ng7-e6+!

Score 5 points.
The knight returns to the centre of

the arena and gives the black king a choice. He can go to e8 and get forked on c7, or he can walk into another discovered check.

19 . . .   Kd8-c8
20 Ne6-c5+

The knight is off on his travels again, looking for new areas to raid.

20 . . .   Kc8-b8

The king can't go back to d8 because 21 Qg4-d7 is mate. He tries to run, but there's nowhere to go!

Q *What does White do now?*

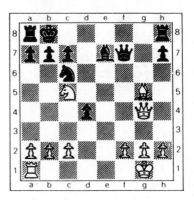

21 Nc5-d7+

Score 3 points.
The knight just goes on hitting and running, hitting and running. This time he sets the black king up for a real beauty.

21 . . .   Kb8-c8

The black king has no choice, he must go where the knight tells him!

Q *How does the knight discover check?*

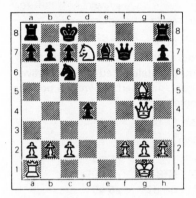

22 Nd7-b6++

Score 4 points.
Score 2 points for 22 Nd7-e5+.
That only wins the queen; the white knight has something more painful in store for Black!

22 ... Kc8-b8

The black king of course still can't go to d8 because of 23 Qg4-d7 mate.

Q *How does White finish off the job?*

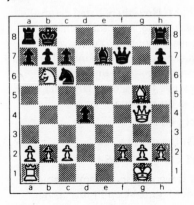

23 Qg4-c8+

Score 3 points.
The knight has finally woven a net around the black king. Black has been forced into a neat form of Philidor's Legacy.

23 ... Rh8xc8
24 Nb6-d7 mate

Morphy gave a tremendous example of how to handle knights on an open board. Without pawn support the knights couldn't dig themselves in on long-term bases; they had to fight a running battle. Black couldn't even find a way to swat at the knights, let alone drive them away. He was too busy saving his king, escaping from discovered checks, and avoiding forks, to develop his rooks and get any sort of control over the vital squares in the centre of his position. The white queen and bishop provided help, and the climax came on move 17 when the knights gave Morphy two different winning variations. After the sacrifice 17 Ng5-f7+ the remaining knight simply drove the black king dizzy! This knight, starting life on b1, moved to c3, e4, g5, e6, g7, e6, c5, d7, and b6, before returning to d7 to deliver the final blow!

The black king's knightmare

The black king yawned. Life could be very tiresome, he thought. He had been stuck in this stupid corner for far too long. It was definitely time for bed.

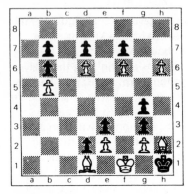

White to move

1 h6-h7

That bishop of his has got to go. . . I can't move anything else anyway! I can't take it myself because 2 h7-h8=Queen and I'm dead.

1 . . .   g3xh2

That's all right now. You can queen your pawn, I'll play . . .g4-g3, and then you can do whatever you like . . .I don't care. . .I'm stalemated, and there's nothing you can do about it. Let's call it a draw and go home.

2 h7-h8=N

A knight? Well, that doesn't make any difference. . .does it?

2 . . .   g4-g3
3 Nh8-g6

Oh I see, perhaps it does.

3 . . .   f7xg6
4 f6-f7   g6-g5

No it doesn't. . .you can queen your pawn, I'll push mine on to g4 and I'm stalemated again. A draw! Great, now perhaps we can both get some sleep.

5 f7-f8=N

Drat!

5 . . .   g5-g4
6 Nf8-e6   d7xe6
7 d6-d7   e6-e5

Look, we've been through all this before!

8 d7-d8=N

Oh really! Not another wretched knight. Why don't you just go away and leave me alone.

8 . . .   e5-e4
9 Nd8-c6

Yes, I guessed you were going there. Waste of time. . .doesn't get you anywhere you know.

9 . . .   b7xc6
10 b5xc6   b6-b5

Right. Now then, listen carefully white king. *I* am threatening to queen my pawn. *You* have got to queen yours to stop me. When you capture my b-pawn I am stalemated. The game is DRAWN. Do you understand?

11 c6-c7

Oh the man's a fool!

11 . . .   b5-b4

If it weren't so uncomfortable I could go to sleep in this corner.

12 c7-c8=N

Mad! He's gone completely mad.

12 ... b4-b3

Now he's got to take the pawn and it's all over. Thank heavens. . . what a bore!

13 Nc8-d6

Ha! He can't stop me from queening. I'm going to win! Ha ha!

13 ... b3-b2

Can't catch me!

14 Nd6xe4 b2-b1=Q

Brilliant. . .it's mate next move. Serves the old fool right. Beautiful . . .I'm going to dream about this. . .

15 Ne4xg3

Aaaagh. . .gulp!

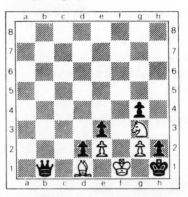

Well, the black king did get something right. It was mate next move!

Born for glory

Some people work hard all their lives and achieve nothing. To others fame and glory seem to fall naturally. Take the black knight for example:

(*King's Gambit*)

1	e2-e4	e7-e5
2	f2-f4	e5xf4
3	b2-b3	Qd8-h4+
4	g2-g3	f4xg3
5	h2-h3	g3-g2+
6	Ke1-e2	Qh4xe4+
7	Ke2-f2	g2xh1=N mate!

The knight, born on move seven, flattens White without even getting out of his cot!

The Austrian, Goetz, won this game in Strasbourg in 1880. His opponent didn't leave his name . . .which judging by the way he played isn't surprising!

Horse-power!

The Concise Oxford Dictionary says horse-power is 'The unit of rate of doing work'. In this position White generates five units and does a fair job of work on the black king!

The position looks messy. Actually it's quite simple.

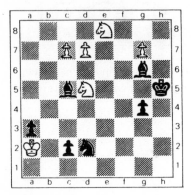

White to move

There are three points to remember, then it is easy:

(a) Black threatens 1 ...c2-c1=N+
    2 Ka2-a1 Nd2-b3 mate.
(b) White can't stop this mate.
(c) Since White can't stop the mate his only chance is to keep checking.

Here's what happened:

1 Nd5-f4+   Kh5-h6

If 1 ...Kh5-g5 (or h4) 2 d7-d8=Q+, and after 3 Qd8xd2 it's all over. Black daren't ever let White queen with check.

2 g7-g8=N+

White steps the work rate up to three horse-power.

2 ...   Kh6-h7
3 Ng8-f6+   Kh7-h6

If 3 ...Kh7-h8, 4 Nf4xg6 is mate.

4 Nf6xg4+   Kh6-h7

Remember, he daren't go to g5.

5 Ne8-f6+   Kh7-g7

He daren't go to h8 either. White still queens the d-pawn with check.

6 Nf4-e6+   Kg7-f7
7 d7-d8=N+

Four horse-power!

7 ...   Kf7-e7
8 c7-c8=N mate

Five horse-power seems to do the job very nicely!

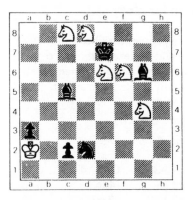

A magnificent mate. The king is surrounded by the horsemen, and each one plays his part!

Combined operations

So far you have had it easy! Well, let's recap on what we have done so far.

First of all we looked at the quick kill. We saw how, by sticking to the rules of the opening, and by developing aggressively, we could keep our opponent under pressure and punish him for his opening mistakes.

Next we looked at open files. We saw how the rooks became stronger when they had open files on which to operate. We saw how the rooks could use the open files to invade the enemy position, and how they became even more powerful if they could safely reach the seventh or eighth ranks.

Then we looked at diagonals. We saw how the position of the pawns affects the scope and power of the bishops. We saw the power of the bishop as a long-range piece, creating and invading holes in the enemy pawn shield.

Finally we looked at the knight. We saw how it fights a hit-and-run battle on an open board, how it can dig itself in on an operations base when there is good pawn cover. We looked at smothered mates and the dangers of the fork.

So far you have had it easy? Well. . . For example, when you were looking at the section on raiding knights you came across four problems to solve. You knew straight away that the winning line must involve using the knight; so you set off looking for the forks, the smothered mates etc! The testgames and problems were chosen to highlight the power of the knight; so you had a big clue before you started — you knew the knights were the important pieces. The same thing applies in the other sections.

In your actual games it won't work like that. At least, not often. Sometimes you will have a game where there is one general theme, but more usually everything will come together. There will be open files, there will be good diagonals, there will be well-placed knights. In most games you will have to tie everything together, make all the pieces work with maximum power. They will have to fight a *combined operation.*

In this section there are two tests. You will get no clues to help you with the Four Problems to Solve. You will have to study the positions and use your knowledge of the power of all the pieces to work out your answer. You will get no clues to help you with the Testgame. Again you will have to work out your answer by considering the power of each and every one of your pieces. You will have to fight a *combined operation.*

TEST FIFTEEN

Four problems to solve

Q *White has to give up his queen to avoid checkmate. How does Black win?*

Q *The white king is in danger. Black can force checkmate. How?*

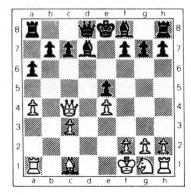

Black to move

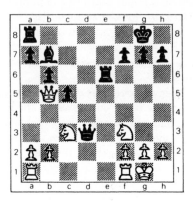

Black to move

The two important points here are the open d-file and White's weakness on his first rank. The black queen must get to d1:

1 . . .   Bd7-b5

Black sacrifices his bishop to clear the way for his queen.
White is lost:

(a)

2 a4xb5   Qd8-d1 mate

(b)

2 Bc1-g5   Bb5xc4+

Black captures the queen with check, White does not have time to capture the black queen.

Score 2 points.

Black has given up a piece for a pawn. His heavy pieces control the central files and his bishop rakes the long diagonal. A queen sacrifice leads to a standard rook-and-bishop mate.

1 . . .   Qd3xf3
2 g2xf3

If White doesn't capture he will simply be mated by the queen on g2.

2 . . .   Re6-g6+
3 Kg1-h1   Bb7xf3 mate

There was no escape for the white king.

Score 3 points.

Q *This time it is the black king who is in danger. How does White force checkmate?*

Q *The threat of mate forces Black to give up a piece. How does White win?*

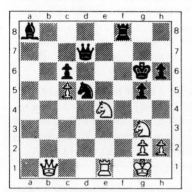

White to move

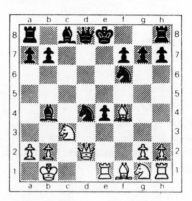

White to move

Black's K-side defences are wrecked, and White's pieces are in position to invade. The important line is the diagonal from b1 to h7 on which White can discover check.

1 Ne4-f6+

There was no way the knight could make use of the discovered check by a direct attack on a black piece.

1 ...   Kg6xf6

If 1 ...Kg6-g7, 2 Qb1-h7+ Kg7xf6 and 3 Ng3-h5 is mate.

2 Ng3-h5+   Kf6-f7
3 Qb1-h7 mate

Note the power of the rook on the open e-file, stopping the king from escaping.

Score 5 points.

The black king is in the centre and the white rook is straining at the leash. White forces open the e-file.

1 Nc3xe4

Black has three main choices:

(a)
1 ...   Bb4xd2
2 Ne4xf6++   Ke8-f8
3 Bf4-d6+   Qd8xd6
4 Re1-e8 mate

(b)
1 ...   Nf6xe4
2 Re1xe4+

And now however Black gets out of check he loses a piece.

(c)
1 ...   Bb4-e7
2 Ne4-d6+   Ke8-f8
3 Qd2xd4

And again White wins a piece.

Score 5 points.

Testgame 15

(*Queen's Gambit Declined*)

Rotlevi	Rubinstein
1 d2-d4	d7-d5
2 Ng1-f3	e7-e6
3 e2-e3	c7-c5
4 c2-c4	Nb8-c6
5 Nb1-c3	Ng8-f6
6 d4xc5	

Weak. White exchanges his centre pawn and gives up any hope of getting a space advantage from the opening.

| 6 ... | Bf8xc5 |

Black recaptures and brings his bishop to life at the same time.

| 7 a2-a3 | a7-a6 |
| 8 b2-b4 | |

Q *What should Black do now?*

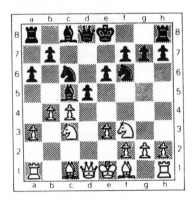

| 8 ... | Bc5-d6 |

Score 3 points.
The bishop moves to its best diagonal, helping to control e5 and aiming at h2. . .which will

soon be part of the white king's pawn shield.

Score 1 point for 8 . . .Bc5-e7. There is no need for the bishop to take up this more defensive position, since there is little likelihood of the white dark-squared bishop coming to g5.

Score 1 point for 8 . . .Bc5-b6, or 8 . . .Bc5-a7. There is not quite so much future for the bishop on this diagonal so long as White keeps his pawn barrier at e3 and f2.

| 9 Bc1-b2 | |

He couldn't win a pawn by 9 c4xd5 e6xd5 10 Nc3xd5 Nf6xd5 11 Qd1xd5 because of 11 . . .Bd6xb4+ when he loses his queen.

9 ...	0-0
10 Qd1-d2	Qd8-e7
11 Bf1-d3	

It was still dangerous for White to grab the pawn: 11 c4xd5 e6xd5 12 Nc3xd5 Nf6xd5 12 Qd2xd5 Bc8-e6 13 Qd5-d1 Nc6xb4 and White is in all sorts of trouble.

Q *What should Black do now?*

11 ...   d5xc4

Score 3 points.
Now that White has moved his
light-squared bishop Black solves
the problem of the centre pawns.
White has to lose a move recapturing.

12 Bd3xc4   b7-b5

Black gains more time.

13 Bc4-d3

The white bishop has been here
before!

Q *What should Black do now?*

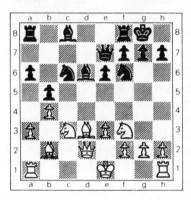

13 ...   Rf8-d8

Score 3 points.
The rook comes to its natural square
on the open file. There may be two
bishops in the way, but the white
queen can't feel safe!

Score 3 points for 13 . . .Bc8-b7.
Developing the bishop on to its
best square on the long diagonal
is just as good.

14 Qd2-e2

The white queen notices the danger!

14 ...   Bc8-b7

Both players have made the same
number of moves, but Black has
made two more than White! Seems
strange, but just look. After fourteen moves the positions of both
players are exactly the same except
that Black has castled and played
. . .Rf8-d8. With this two-move
advantage Black has clearly won the
battle of the opening, and will be
first to launch his middle-game
attack.

15 0-0

Q *What should Black do now?*

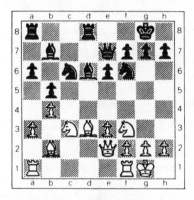

15 ...   Nc6-e5!

Score 4 points.
Black goes to war, and his knight
leads the troops. There are two
main threats. One is to smash up
White's castled position by capturing on f3, the other is to win the
white queen by capturing on d3:
16 . . .Ne5xd3 17 Qe2xd3 Bd6xh2+.
Score 2 points for 15 . . .Ra8-c8.

16 Nf3xe5

White gets rid of the annoying
knight. But this was the main pur-
pose of Black's last move: to ex-

change knights: to destroy White's best K-side defender!

16	...	Bd6xe5
17	f2-f4	Be5-c7
18	e3-e4	

Q *What should Black do now?*

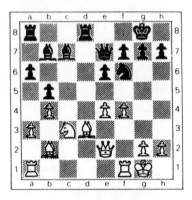

18 ...   Ra8-c8

Score 4 points.
Develop first. . .attack later!
Black's rook takes the second open file, and now all his pieces are in play.

Score 1 point for 18 . . . Bc7-b6+.
There is no hurry to commit your bishop to this diagonal.
Score 1 point for 18 . . .e6-e5.
This bold central strike holds up the white e-pawn, but allows White to close the centre up with f4-f5. Black will then have a nasty hole on d5, and his better-placed pieces will lose the freedom of an open board.

19   e4-e5

White dislodges the black knight, but in doing so he opens the long diagonal for Black's light-squared bishop.

19	...	Bc7-b6+
20	Kg1-h1	

Q *What should Black do now?*

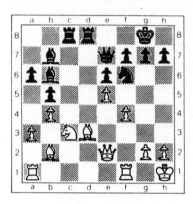

20 ...   Nf6-g4

Score 4 points.
Black gives White a choice. White can either leave this knight where it is and let it raid his K-side, or he can capture it and let the black rooks loose down the centre.

Score 1 point for 20 . . .Nf6-d5.

21   Bd3-e4

Q *What should Black do now?*

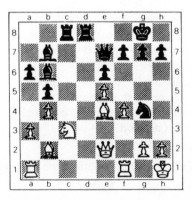

21 ...   Qe7-h4

Score 4 points.

22 g2-g3

White beats off the mate threat, at the cost of opening up his king.

Q *What should Black do now?*

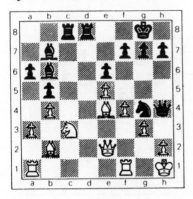

22 ...   Rc8xc3!!

Score 0 points.

Yes, 0 points! If you found that move you cheated!

23 g3xh4

What else? 23 Bb2xc3 Bb7xe4+ leads to mate, and 23 Be4xb7 Rc3xg3 is just as bad.

Q *What should Black do now?*

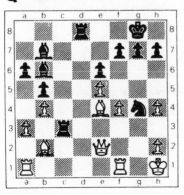

23 ...   Rd8-d2!!

Score 6 points.

Absolutely brilliant! The rooks have simply smashed their way down the open files into the enemy position. They are superbly supported by the bishops, which supply a blistering cross-fire, and the knight which thumps h2. Black is a queen down, and four of his five pieces are *en prise*, but that doesn't matter ...it's the white king who's got the problems!

24 Qe2xd2

Again, what else? Quick mate follows 24 Qe2xg4 Bb7xe4+, or 24 Bb2xc3 Rd2xe2, or 24 Be4xb7 Rd2xe2 25 Bb7-g2 Rc3-h3.

24 ...   Bb7xe4+

25 Qd2-g2

Q *What should Black do now?*

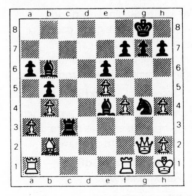

25 ...   Rc3-h3!

Score 4 points.

In the last four moves the whole black army has exploded with colossal power. Devastating. Brilliant Rubinstein. White of course resigned!

TEST SIXTEEN

Four problems to solve

Q *The black king cannot survive White's attack. How does White force checkmate?*

Q *Again the black king is in trouble, and again White can force checkmate. How?*

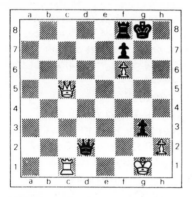

White to move

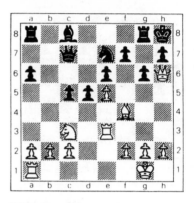

White to move

The white queen would look pretty on g7: she can't get there though! The queen *can* force her way to the back rank, and that is where Black's biggest trouble lies.

1 Qc5xf8+   Kg8xf8

If the king tries to run away then the white queen does get to g7: 1 ...Kg8-h7 2 Qf8-g7 mate.

2 Rc1-c8+   Qd2-d8
3 Rc8xd8 mate

Score 2 points.

The black rook is ready to come to the rescue by defending h7. White must use the h-file to strike immediately.

1 Qh6xh7+   Kh8xh7
2 Re3-h3+   Kh7-g7
3 Bf4-h6+

The bishop pounces on to the diagonal and forces the black king back to the h-file.

3 ...   Kg7-h7 (or h8)
4 Bh6-f8 mate

Discovered attack on the open file!

Score 3 points.

Q *Now it is White's turn to suffer! How does Black force checkmate?*

Q *Again it is the white king who is mated. How?*

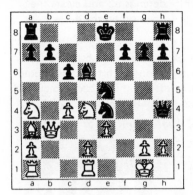

Black to move

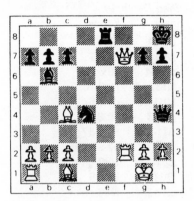

Black to move

White's pieces seem to have gone off their majesty! Black's are in position to make a closer inspection!

1 ...   Qh4xh2+

A queen sacrifice! White has a choice: take, or run away.

(a)
2 Kg1xh2   Ne5-f3++

And now, if 3 Kh2-h1 or 3 Kh2-h3 Ne4-f2 is mate.

(b)
2 Kg1-f1   Qh2-h1+
3 Kf1-e2   Qh1xg2+
4 Ke2-e1   Qg2-f2 mate

The knights hold all the power!

Score 4 points.

Black wins this with all his pieces playing a part. First he uses the open e-file and invades the back rank:

1 ...   Re8-e1+

White has a choice:

(a)
2 Rf2-f1   Nd4-f3++

The knight both checks and discovers check!

3 Kg1-h1   Qh4xh2 mate.

(b)
2 Bc4-f1   Nd4-e2+

This time the knight raids alone!

3 Kg1-h1   Re1xf1+

The white rook is now forced off f2, allowing the black bishop to cover g1.

4 Rf2xf1   Ne2-g3 mate

A neat, almost smothered mate!

Score 6 points.

Testgame 16

(*Sicilian Defence*)

Ravinski   Panov

1	e2-e4	c7-c5
2	Ng1-f3	e7-e6
3	d2-d4	c5xd4
4	Nf3xd4	Ng8-f6
5	Nb1-c3	d7-d6
6	g2-g3	Nb8-c6
7	Bf1-g2	Bc8-d7
8	0-0	a7-a6
9	Bc1-e3	Ra8-c8
10	Qd1-e2	b7-b5
11	a2-a3	Nc6-e5

Q *What should White do now?*

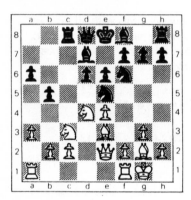

12 Ra1-d1

Score 2 points.

Black obviously intends to move his knight to c4, attacking White's bishop, and raiding the Q-side. White develops his rook on to the open line and makes way for his bishop to retreat to c1. If Black wastes too much time with his knight White may get the chance for a sharp attack in the centre.

12	...	Ne5-c4
13	Be3-c1	

White defends b2 and clears the way for action on the e-file.

13	...	Nc4xa3?

Black grabs a pawn, but he's wasting too much time. He should have left his knight back on c6 and played . . . Bf8-e7 and . . . 0-0.

Q *What should White do now?*

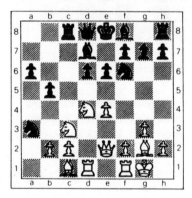

14 e4-e5

Score 3 points.

Black is behind in development; his king is still in the centre. White's queen and rook stand powerfully on the centre files. White seizes his chance to smash open the centre.

No score for other moves. 14 b2xa3 Rc8xc3 leaves White's Q-side in tatters, and is particularly bad.

14	...	d6xe5

Black doesn't have much choice. If 14 . . .Nf6-d5 15 Nc3xd5 and his knight on a3 is lost.

Q *What should White do now?*

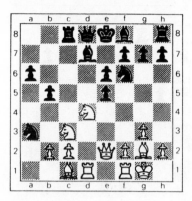

15 Nd4-c6!

Score 4 points.
The knight makes use of the pin on the open d-file to raid enemy territory.

Score 1 point for 15 Qe2xe5. This isn't so good because the queen gets driven off by 15 . . .Na3-c4.

15 . . .   Qd8-c7
16 Nc6xe5   Na3-c4

Q *What should White do now?*

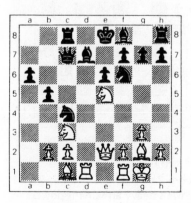

17 Ne5xd7

Score 3 points.
After this capture White's light-squared bishop can rule the long diagonal from h1 to a8 completely unchallenged. At the same time Black's king position becomes slightly more perilous. One of his royal guards has gone, and his control of e6 has been weakened.

No score for 17 Ne5xc4 when White gets very little for his pawn.
Score 1 point for 17 Bc1-f4.

17 . . .   Nf6xd7

Another advantage of White's last move is that Black has to re-capture with this knight, with-drawing the piece from the centre.

Q *What should White do now?*

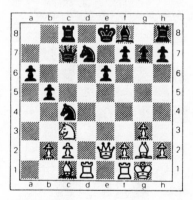

18 Nc3-d5

Score 3 points.
White's command of the centre is growing every move. He uses his control of the centre files to improve the position of his knight.

Combined operations

Score 1 point for 18 f2-f4. The idea of playing the pawn on to f5 and smashing open more files is good, but too slow. Black replies with 18 . . .Bf8-c5+ and 19 . . .0-0. *Score 1 point* for 18 Rf1-e1.

18 ...   Qc7-a7
19 Nd5-f4

The pawn on e6 is the barrier to White's attack on the centre files. If this can be dynamited Black's whole defences will crumble, and the rest will be a massacre.

19 ...   Nc4-e5

Black tries to hold the position by blocking the road to e6. He would probably have done better to have tried 19 . . .Bf8-e7 and faced the storm.

Q *What should White do now?*

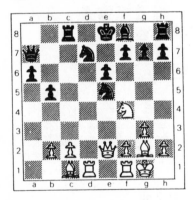

20 Rd1xd7!

Score 5 points.
White begins the job of demolishing Black's position.

20 ...   Ne5xd7

Q *What should White do now?*

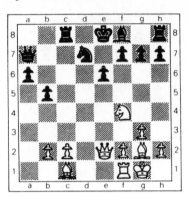

21 Nf4xe6!
Score 5 points.
The draught blows cold around Black's king!

21 ...   f7xe6
22 Qe2xe6+ Bf8-e7

Q *What should White do now?*

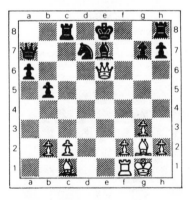

23 Rf1-e1
Score 2 points.
White's heavy armament powers down the open file threatening

mate on e7. His bishops lurk in the background, waiting to unleash their fury on the open board.

Score 1 point for 23 Bc1-g5. This is not so good because Black replies 23 . . .Qa7-c5, defending the mate threat and attacking the bishop.

23 . . .   Qa7-c5
24 b2-b4!

White tries to lure the black queen off c5 so that he can play 25 Bc1-g5.

24 . . .   Nd7-f8
25 Qe6-g4

White withdraws: for the moment the black king seems to have found safety behind his bishop.

25 . . .   Qc5-c3

Black saves his queen and manages to guard c8 and g7 at the same time. He threatens White's rook and so prevents 26 Bc1-g5.

Q *What should White do now?*

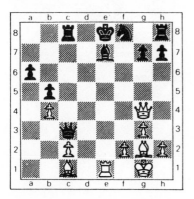

26 Re1xe7+!

Score 5 points.
Each time a black piece gets between White and his goal it is

blasted away.

26 . . .   Ke8xe7
27 Bc1-g5+

The bishops have waited in the wings for long enough. Now they come into their own: an open board and beautiful diagonals.

27 . . .   Ke7-d6

Q *What should White do now?*

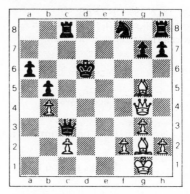

28 Qg4-d1+

Score 3 points.
This is the only route to checkmate. White must play accurately. It is no use just checking the black king around the board and hoping for the best. Black has a big lead in material; he would win if his queen could come to the defence and stave off White's attack. Black, in fact, resigned at this point. . .which isn't surprising as he is being mated:

28 . . .   Kd6-c7

If 28 . . .Kd6-e6, 29 Qd1-d5 is mate.

29 Bg5-f4+   Kc7-b6
30 Qd1-d6+   Kb6-a7

If 30 . . .Rc8-c6, 31 Qd6-b8 is mate.

31 Qd6-e7+   Rc8-c7

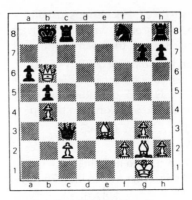

Position after 34 Qd8-b6 mate

If 31 . . .Ka7-b6, 32 Qe7-b7 is mate.

32 Bf4-e3+   Ka7-b8

If 32 . . .Qc3xe3, 33 Qe7xc7 is mate.

33 Qe7-d8+   Rc7-c8
34 Qd8-b6 mate

Piece power!

Raiding knights hitting and running.

Rooks seizing open files.

The enemy defences demolished.

The enemy king on the run.

Bishops sweeping across open diagonals.

The queen, majestic on an open board.

The enemy king cornered.

The execution!

Piece power . . . at its best.

Index of openings